Satish Kumar: Abundant Love

Part of the Longform Conversations series

Series Editor: Jagdish Rattanani

Satish Kumar: Abundant Love

by Jagdish Rattanani

with Sudarshan Iyengar and Lisa Pearson

Triarchy Press

Published by:
Triarchy Press
Axminster, England

First edition: 2023

info@triarchypress.net
www.triarchypress.net

A catalogue record is available from the British Library.

Cover image: copyright © Jyoti Sahi

ISBNs:

Paperback: 978-1-913743-70-3
eBook: 978-1-913743-71-0

To my parents, who brought me up with abundant love, and my parents-in-law, who showered more love on me.

Jagdish Rattanani, Series Editor

The cover image is taken from a silk screen print by Jyoti Sahi, who is a practising artist and writer concerned with symbols important in Indian culture. This graphic symbol of a seed is depicted with a *chakravyuha*, or Indian labyrinth, embedded in its layered form.

The artist found this ritual maze in a folk shrine in what is now the protected area of the Bannerghatta National Park near Bengaluru – the city that has grown to become India's software services hub. The labyrinth in the shrine is marked out with stones, delineating a path that leads to its centre. Local pilgrims walk this labyrinth in the belief that it will bring life's blessings to the family in the birth of a child.

The seed symbolises the promise of life. The labyrinth holds the secret to life, which is like a maze enfolding the Divine Presence hidden at its centre. The act of walking into the labyrinth performs a ritual process of uncovering the embodied *atma*, or Self, lying at the seed's heart.

Jyoti Sahi made this design inspired by the ecological movement that ensures the diversity of native seeds, sustaining the life of the community.

~~~

The images of Satish Kumar on pages 24, 50, 98 and 197 were taken at the time of these conversations at Vandana Shiva's Navdanya farm in Dehradun, Northern India.

Contents

FOREWORD 1:

Reverential Ecology

By Charles Eisenstein

In these interviews Satish Kumar invokes the concept of reverential ecology. Whereas deep ecology, as articulated by Arne Næss, steps beyond instrumentalist views to say that nature and all its beings have intrinsic value, regardless of their usefulness, reverential ecology takes a further step. It sees nature – all life, all beings – as sacred.

Reverential ecology is already implicit in deep ecology, for what is this 'intrinsic value' of which it speaks? The modern mind, conditioned by market economies, hardly understands value apart from transaction, from the equation of one thing with another. Intrinsic value means value independent of utility or exchange. To the modern mind it is nearly an oxymoron. Naturally then, we reach for a concept other than value to express what deep ecology is really reaching toward; hence, sacredness and reverence.

In other words, reverential ecology is not actually a step beyond deep ecology at all. It is what deep ecology actually is and must be. It says there is more to existence than what we can use and what we can count. Herein lies Satish Kumar's insight, which bears a close relation to the trajectory of his life.

What is this other thing, that cannot be reduced to numbers? The usual answer is 'spirit', but this answer falls short of reverence, for it holds things sacred for what they have rather than what they are. Matter is still profane, but for this extra ingredient. This view leads ultimately to precisely the unworldliness that Satish Kumar rejected when he chose to leave the monastic order.

As he describes it in this book, the purpose of the Jain monk is to extinguish all karma so as to be liberated from the material world. In this, as in standard economic thinking, the world has no intrinsic value, only a utilitarian value, an exchange value. Modern market economies tend to reduce all things to money, subsuming the whole world under market relations. It is quite understandable that, as more and more of the world turns into product and property, one should hope to escape the world to find the sacred. Another path, though, would be to reclaim the world from the market. Not, perhaps, to abolish the market, but to reverse its totalising tendencies and limit it to its proper domain, and in so doing protect and expand the realm of the unquantified and the unowned, the commons and the gift. Herein lies a link between the economic philosophy of E.F. Schumacher and the spiritual path of Satish Kumar.

The sacred is not to be found by reducing something to its elemental components and identifying one of them as spirit... It is rather a property of relationships and of wholes

This path seeks sacredness within the world, not outside it. It stands in contrast not only to transcendentalist religious philosophies, but also to modern science and economics, each of which subordinates quality to quantity and reduces relationship to number. The sacred is not to be found by reducing something to its elemental components and identifying one of them as spirit, alongside other ingredients like protons and electrons. It is rather a property of relationships and of wholes. Therefore, the quest for the sacred takes one deeper into relationship to the world.

The repudiation of worldly ties bears a subtle kinship to a perverse unworldliness at the centre of modern economy and technology. Oft-criticised for being too materialistic, they are rather (from the perspective of reverential ecology) not materialistic enough. They treat matter as if it didn't matter. They do not apprehend the holiness of the material world; accordingly, they treat it as profane, valuable only for its usefulness, something to rise above. It is not only religion that enshrines the non-worldly; secular society too accords high prestige or wealth to those who operate entirely in abstractions, such as theoretical physicists and hedge fund managers. What would our society look like if we chose to really take our materialism seriously? If we aspired to make the material world as beautiful and alive as we could? If we treasured the world and everything in it, and sought to serve its highest expression?

This is not to say that 'usefulness' is a lower order of value, something we should spurn in our quest for the sacred. That is how dualistic thinking creeps back in, riding the perverse modern disdain for matter. In the end, reverence for matter redounds to its usefulness. To take for example one of Satish's main subjects of passion, the soil, it is simply untrue that treating it with reverence makes it less useful. To the short-sighted it may seem to bring greater yield and profit to strip the soil through industrial agriculture, but that is an illusion. In the long run, what is good for the soil is good for ourselves.

ultimately, we are not separate from the soil, or indeed from any being on this Earth

Why should that be? It is because ultimately, we are not separate from the soil, or indeed from any being on this Earth. It may seem to the modern mind that the depletion of biodiversity needn't harm humanity. After all, civilization has been depleting biodiversity for thousands of years (accelerating in recent centuries to industrial pace), but humans are just fine, aren't they? There are more of us and less of everything else.

Yes, assessed by the numbers that may be true, but what about the things that escape measure? There are more of us than ever, and we are wealthier and consume more, but are we happier? Are we more content? Are we less afraid? Do we feel a strong sense of community and belonging? The fact is, when a species goes extinct, something dies within ourselves. When a forest you loved is clearcut, can you not feel the inner desolation too? When the soil is depleted, is it any wonder that human health deteriorates?

These examples point to an underlying unity of usefulness and sacredness, of reverence and practicality.

Our civilization has conceptually, through science, and practically, through technology and industry, attempted to take apart nature and build paradise from its parts. This Babelian attempt to build a tower to heaven has attained dizzying heights, yet we seem no closer to paradise. Maybe we have it backwards. Maybe we discover paradise by seeing the world as already sacred. If so, we might see in Satish Kumar's life a map for our society's path forward: to fully embrace the world whose sacredness we once repudiated, to strengthen the dependencies we once sought to transcend, and to seek to leave the world more alive and beautiful than it was when we entered it.

Charles Eisenstein speaks and writes on themes of civilization, consciousness, money, and human cultural evolution. He is the author of *Sacred Economics* and *Ascent of Humanity*.

FOREWORD 2:

Satish Kumar's Experiments with Truth

By Arun Maira

I met Satish Kumar at my mother's breakfast table on a cold winter morning in New Delhi. Satish had stayed overnight with the family on his way to Dehradun. My mother's living room was not heated. Satish was cold. He had draped my mother's shawl around his shoulders. Vandana Shiva, to whose institution, Navdanya in Dehradun, Satish was travelling, was a good friend of both my mother and Satish. Vandana was a frequent visitor to my mother's home, always wearing a large bindi*, on her forehead and her own beautiful shawls. Navdanya gathers and preserves the seeds of traditional plants. My mother was the honorary vice-chancellor of the 'grandmothers' university' in Navdanya, which Vandana had formed to gather and celebrate traditional knowledge of food and cooking and mothers' care for children.

I was delighted to meet Satish, having read his books and articles in *Resurgence*, copies of which were on my mother's bookshelves. I have read many great thinkers in *Resurgence*, including Satish himself, Vandana Shiva, Fritjof Capra and E.F. Schumacher, the founder of *Resurgence*, who had persuaded Satish to become the editor of the magazine. Satish is one of the longest serving editors of any magazine in the world, having edited *Resurgence* for 43 years.

Satish wore his wisdom as light-heartedly as he had draped the shawl around himself. Though our meeting was brief, his unassuming manner has left a lasting impression on me.

---

*terms marked with an asterisk are further explained in the Glossary (p.179)

Sudarshan Iyengar and Jagdish Rattanani were fortunate to have more time with Satish than I had. They talked with him for many hours over several days in Navdanya. They have recorded their 'long-form interview' in this book. It was a great pleasure for me to read it and understand Satish's thoughts more deeply, as well as to know Satish the human being more fully, which I could not in my brief encounter at my mother's breakfast table.

My mother's library was filled with books about Mahatma Gandhi and with Gandhiji's own writings. My mother and Satish shared a deep respect for Gandhiji. I was drawn to Gandhiji too. My mother would remind me often, when I would borrow a Gandhi book from her, that Gandhiji had actually touched my head. When I was four years old, she had taken me to Gandhiji's prayer meeting in Delhi, a few days before he was assassinated. When the crowds rushed to get his personal blessings, Gandhiji asked that the little children be allowed to come closest to him. Then he touched my head and blessed me. "Never forget that", my mother would say.

I hear Gandhiji in Satish's life and his thoughts. Readers of this wonderful dialogue will too. But they will find much more. Jagdish and Sudarshan have wrapped the dialogue in two wonderful 'covers', one by each of them. Through them, one can see what has touched them the most, like lasting impressions on a tissue wrapped around a sweet. My foreword is another wrapper around theirs. It carries impressions from both, the wonderful dialogue itself, and their covers around it. Here are some ideas of Satish's that have left the strongest impressions on me.

A journey from inner being to helping the world to become

The first are connections between 'being' and 'becoming', which Sudarshan sees too, in his cover, 'The Long Walk: From Being to Becoming'. Satish chose to become a Jain* monk when he was a young boy. He went through a gruelling initiation (as hazardous as any hazing in a college fraternity!) Jain monks must learn to keep themselves pure, free from violence against any creature – they must not even pluck fleas that infect their bodies – as Satish learned in his initiation. If any violence must be done to protect a monk or feed a monk, others must do it for him. Because a monk must keep his own self pure.

The young Satish soon realised that this was a form of escapism from reality and even a form of extreme selfishness. He became drawn to the ideas of Mahatma Gandhi, and his close disciple Vinoba Bhave. Their lives were long journeys of self-purification, as well as actions to improve the world for others, especially those most oppressed by others. Their life-long journeys were not the walks of mendicant monks, expecting others to drop food in their bowls, so that they would not have to work to earn and pay for it, or even to cook it. Their long walks, like Gandhiji's Dandi March, and Vinoba's treks through India, were to walk with people and lead them in fights for their own freedoms; or to demand that others give freedom to oppressed people (such as Bhave's 'bhoodan'* – the voluntary donations of land by rich landlords to landless peasants). They were helping the world to become better, while also purifying themselves. Gandhiji called his autobiography, *The Story of My Experiments with Truth.*

This book is a story of Satish Kumar's experiments with truth.

The purposes of our lives

Those who choose not to withdraw from the world but to act, confront the question, 'What is the purpose of my life?' For a monk who has withdrawn completely into self-purification, the purpose of living is self-improvement only. However, for those who choose to act to improve the world also, hubris can set in.

The belief that humans are God's chosen species, created in 'God's own image' – and even that some amongst them are God's chosen people – has made some humans believe it is their God-given right to lord it over nature and over others.

The European Enlightenment released the powers of science and technology, the handmaiden of science. These have given humans great power over nature and other species, and some nations power over others. Tragically, human wisdom has not matured as fast as new technologies have developed. In fact, the wisdom that ancients had before science, that humans are a small piece of nature, and not its master, has been lost.

Robert Frost, the poet, says to God that God must forgive all Frost's 'little jokes' on God if Frost forgives God for his 'great big joke' on Frost! The great big joke is to give humans the belief that they have power over God's natural world. No other species seems to have this belief. They take the world as it is and fit themselves into it. Humans, however, want to change nature to make life more comfortable for themselves.

Technology, economy and business

Technology is used to create machines and automobiles, to build big dams, to clear forests, level the earth, and build tall cities. Technology makes the economy grow. GDP increases. Nature is in pain from the economy's heavy footprint on the Earth. It is heating up. Scientists are looking for 'scientific' and technological solutions to climate change and environmental distress. These also will add to GDP. Destroy with technology on one hand; repair with technology on the other. The greater the economic activity, regardless of whether it is beneficial or harmful, the faster it builds GDP. This makes economists and business people happy, though the planet suffers, and people also suffer.

'Planet, Profit and People' has become a slogan for businesses. Many claim they are concerned about all three. However, when they have to take decisions, profit always comes first. For many it is the only thing that matters. After all, the business of business must be to make profits because that is how business serves society best, declared Milton Friedman in the *New York Times* in September 1970.

Some business professors have been trying to persuade business leaders to give equal attention to all three – Planet, Profit and People. They say that, ultimately, this will be good for business. They present studies to show that companies that care for people and the planet create more shareholder wealth in the long run. The ultimate measure of the success of a business, they would suggest, is the amount of financial wealth it creates.

The soul's satisfaction provides a 'peace that passeth all understanding'; a peace that economists cannot even measure.

Satish Kumar offers an alternative alliteration to 'Planet, Profits and People'. It is, 'Soil, Soul and Society'. The difference in the middle is significant. Whereas 'soil and society' and 'planet and people' can be synonymous, satisfaction of the soul is very different to money in the bank. The soul's satisfaction provides a 'peace that passeth all understanding'; a peace that economists cannot even measure.

Satish says that, as human civilisation moved from respecting nature to growing economies, and then on to worshipping money, the science of 'ecology' moved to the science of 'economy', and, in the last thirty years, 'economy' has transformed to 'money-nomy'! The condition of economies is judged by what stock-market investors and financial investors think of them. Every morning, investors around the world nervously wait for the ringing of the bell on the New York Stock Exchange to know whether the world is doing better or worse than the day before. The conditions of homeless people a few blocks from the New York exchange, and the much larger numbers of homeless people sleeping just outside the Bombay Stock Exchange, do not appear on the high-frequency measures that wealthy people track, nor do they appear on the dashboards of governments who compete to attract investors.

Systems thinking

Humanity cannot carry on the way it is. The impact of the Covid pandemic around the world has made it clear that we need new instruments on the dashboard. We need new scorecards that report the condition of all people, not just the rich. We must listen to forests, rivers, oceans and even the air we breathe. All nations have accepted that the UN's Sustainable Development Goals are a better scorecard of the health of the whole system than GDP and stock prices are.

Satish points out that change will not be easy. Changes to established paradigms, which give the establishment its power and wealth, will be resisted, as Thomas Kuhn explained in *The Structure of Scientific Revolutions*.

How are large complex systems transformed? Nature shows how. When an ecology changes, many things in it change together – the plants, the animals, the soil, even the micro-climate. Because all parts of an ecology need each other. Albert Einstein said that it is madness to attempt to solve problems with the same approach that caused them. Modern science cannot provide the solution, because modern science has created the systemic problem that needs to be solved. The European Enlightenment unleashed science and technology onto the world. Sciences became more specialised as they advanced. Individual scientists know more and more about less and less. They have lost sight of how everything works together.

We need to apply 'systems science' to find systemic solutions to systemic problems. Systems science is the science of relationships. It explains that systems have 'emergent' properties which cannot be seen in the properties of their constituent parts. The physicist Fritjof Capra (Satish's friend and contributor to *Resurgence*), and Pier Luigi Luisi, a professor of biochemistry, give an excellent exposition of systems thinking in their book, *The Systems View of Life: A Unifying Vision*. They extend the view of systems beyond the physical sciences. They explain how the

Satish Kumar: Abundant Love

'emergent' property of human consciousness can arise from biological and social configurations.

His Holiness the Dalai Lama is a deep meditator, devoted, as a Buddhist monk should be, to self-purification. He was compelled to break out of his retreat in Lhasa, to engage with the politics of power in the world. He has been on a long personal journey of transformation of self *and* society. He has explored insights from Western science with the best Western scientists who, in turn, have been exploring with him ideas from Eastern spiritual traditions. The Dalai Lama explains his insights in *The Universe in a Single Atom: The Convergence of Science and Spirituality.*

There are some parallels in the quests of both Satish and the Dalai Lama. Both are on journeys of exploration of the self *and* society. As was Gandhiji, whom both admire.

Communities of change

Finally, to brass tacks. How can we break out of the gold shackles with which ideas of progress have become enslaved, as human civilisation has morphed from an ecology to a 'money-nomy'? Capitalism is too deeply entrenched, Satish says. Money runs politics; it runs the media; it funds think-tanks. Money rules the world. How can people without money change the world when they do not have the power of money to support them?

Satish says those who want to make the world better for everyone must create alternatives first, rather than banging their heads against walls that resist them. That's how nature evolves. As the new emerges, the old fades. Change in complex systems has to be an organic process, not a large-scale 're-engineering' exercise. Blueprints of new solutions will emerge from small changes in many places.

When E. F. Schumacher wrote *Small is Beautiful: Economics as if People Mattered* in 1973, he was derided as a romanticist. In a world enamoured with 'large-scale solutions' – large factories, large economies, large dams and large armies, 'small' seemed silly. Gandhiji's ideas about village enterprises and villages as sites for human and ecological harmony had also been set aside twenty years earlier when India joined the rest of the world to build 'commanding heights' in its economy – big factories and big dams.

The science of economics took a turn after *Small is Beautiful* was published. Friedman and his colleagues in the Chicago School of

Economics rewrote Keynesian economics to say profits and money mattered in economics and people did not count as much.

A new paradigm of economics is required in which people matter more than profits. Schumacher wrote in *Resurgence*, in 1968:

> *What is the meaning of democracy, freedom, human dignity, standard of living, self-realization, fulfillment? Is it a matter of goods, or of people? Of course, it is a matter of people. But people can be themselves only in small comprehensible groups. Therefore, we must learn to think in terms of an articulated structure that can cope with a multiplicity of small-scale units.*

Complex systems composed of a diversity of forces – natural, human and economic – come together in unique shapes in different localities. The shape of the socio-ecological system is not the same in the slums of Mumbai, the Amazon rainforests, the steppes of Russia or in Manhattan. Therefore, solutions by the world's best experts working in remote centres of large organisations – in government, international development organisations and large multinationals – cannot fit everyone. Standardisation can produce efficiency and it can help to deliver solutions at scale. However, standard solutions delivered at scale are very often the wrong solutions for most people; and especially for the poorest people. They are considered inferior because they are poor. And they are expected to swallow bad advice because that is what their benefactors insist they must accept.

...people want dignity. Therefore, they must be the agents of their own wellbeing, not mere recipients of others' charity

The world must adopt a radically different approach to solve the systemic problems of sustainable development goals. *Local systems solutions, collaboratively implemented by communities, are necessary to solve systemic global problems.* Small is the solution to the problems caused by the big. Ultimately, the wellbeing of people matters, not the GDP. Moreover, people want dignity. Therefore, they must be the agents of their own wellbeing, not mere recipients of others' charity.

Long walks to freedom

A more just, and more resilient, world order will not be built in the lifetimes of even the greatest human beings. Gandhiji's work remains unfinished.

Across the Indian Ocean, in South Africa, where Gandhiji discovered the importance of human dignity, the country is descending into despair after the great hope with which it appeared on the world stage as the 'rainbow nation' in 1994. Nelson Mandela's 'long march to freedom' must be carried on by a new generation. They must overcome the new black establishment that has arisen after the old white one was dissolved, says Jay Naidoo, who fought for the freedom of all workers (and black Africans) for decades and who was a minister in Mandela's cabinet. '*Pole, pole*' [slowly, slowly, step-by-step] we must keep walking, Naidoo says, in his book, *Change: Creating Tomorrow Today.*

'*Charaiveti, charaiveti*' [keep walking], says Satish Kumar.

Arun Maira is the Chairman of HelpAge International, a former member of India's Planning Commission and the author of several books. Among them are the following titles published in India: *Transforming Systems: Why The World Needs A New Ethical Toolkit; Transforming Capitalism;* and *A Billion Fireflies: Critical Conversations to Shape a New Post-pandemic World.*

COVER 1:

'Oh, those people who want to change the world!'

By Jagdish Rattanani

Are we in charge of our lives or is there a hidden hand leading us to a destination we know not? It is an eternal question, simple and innocent at one level; complex and profound at another, when probed from the many dimensions of life it opens up. This book is an unlikely journey that totters between planned and unplanned, action and happenstance, pushing and letting go. A set of coincidences took me to Ashridge Business School and then to Schumacher College, where I felt an urge to meet Satish Kumar. That says nothing much because, after all, who does not want to meet Satish Kumar when visiting Schumacher. He was not on campus while I was there in 2015, so the meeting never happened, and was unlikely to take place any time soon as I returned to India. It did eventually happen, in India, in Dehradun, in the farm run by the redoubtable Vandana Shiva, where she does the work of preserving seeds as our living heritage for humanity. The meeting was arranged thanks to the efforts of Lisa Pearson, friend, researcher and horticultural therapist.

Satish Kumar is not well-known in India. He is better known in the West and is a leading light in the eco-spiritual movement that is getting increasing attention across the world as we begin to come to terms with the full implications of the destruction of our environment. He does not carry conventional university degrees, but his life has been one of ongoing action and inquiry, a journey that has brought him wisdom of the kind not easily found. He has used all of it to reimagine teaching and learning at a place that has a historic connection with India, Schumacher College in Devon, which Satish helped found. The college sits on a part of the Dartington Hall estate, which was inspired by Rabindranath Tagore and founded in the 1920s by a secretary of Tagore's, Leonard Elmhirst, and his wife Dorothy – "two of the most romantic figures in English society" according to the *Dundee Courier* (Men and Women of Today, 1929). Satish is also one of the longest-serving editors in the world, leading *Resurgence* magazine and building on a legacy that goes back to E. F. Schumacher as the founder-editor. Satish was a child-monk who lived, as all Jain monks do, on alms. And then, quite remarkably for a Jain monk, he fled his order to became a peace activist, and then a champion of simple living anchored, literally, in the soil.

To Satish, there seems to be no greater crime, no greater tragedy, than parting a man from his land and soil

This book is an exploration of Satish Kumar's knowledge and insights, and a bit of wondering aloud on how his idea of 'elegant simplicity', as he likes to call it, might work in a world we like to see as complex. The questions here are as student, sceptic, even naysayer, steeped as most of us are in a GDP-everything economy from which it appears hard to escape. My fellow interviewer Dr. Sudarshan Iyengar and I also gently push into the socio-political domain, where we seek to draw Satish to comment on the thoughts of Babasaheb Ambedkar*, the leader who fought for the dignity and rights of the millions of 'backwards' in India's caste-ridden* society, and who supported their migration to the cities to escape upper-caste exploitation in what Ambedkar called their village 'ghettos'. Rooted in the sacredness of soil as he is, Satish Kumar finds it appalling that a people should move from their villages, whatever the circumstances, and choose urban squalor instead. To him, there seems to be no greater crime, no greater tragedy, than parting a man from his land and soil. This is a topic that will need deeper exploration.

Satish was kind, bore everything we heaped on him, and in fact took special steps to keep aside time to engage with us. Sometimes he would walk into our simple room on the Dehradun campus called Navdanya and sit on the cot, speaking to us till late into the evening. One day he met us at the small but elegant Navdanya library, and at other times we sat in the open on the campus for our interview sessions.

The result is presented here as a 'long-form conversation', the first in a series that we hope to run with many others in our effort to play with ideas that are rich and often lost in the everyday busyness of our lives. Through this conversation we hope to take Satish Kumar's voice to new audiences, and to introduce more people to his ideas by framing them in the context of the world today.

We, of course, find Satish Kumar's ideas remarkable, but are his ways practical – to go back to basics, grow your own food and live happily ever after? How do you even imagine a world where there are few or no flights, where big businesses are shut, where consumption as we have grown to know it comes to an almost complete standstill, where the shopping malls are empty and where the local becomes the world so that we can begin to rediscover and delight in our own homes, neighbours and neighbour-hoods? How is that even possible?

Then, not long after we did the interviews, exactly such a situation came to be. The lockdowns following the outbreak of the COVID 19 pandemic brought us a world very different from the one built on the mental and economic models that told us more is good, bigger is better, and getting there faster is best. The lockdowns can help us build a new narrative about development, the forced slowing down giving us the time to reflect on, revisit and rebuild some of our ideas of what constitutes good living. Will the pandemic actually deliver this change, or was it merely a blip – one at a huge human cost, though – in mankind's well-entrenched conventional path of 'progress'?

In this conventional ecosystem, a young student, full of energy and willing to exert himself, or a manager assessed by the results she delivers quarter after quarter, is pushed to deliver on the immediate, short-term goal at hand, and to somehow cross the 'hurdles' on that path. And the only way we learn how to go about it is to use every resource for the immediate outcome that must result, using some variant of the so-called Colin Powell doctrine of 'decisive force in order to overcome the enemy' – which in fact is not the complete reading of the doctrine. But the metaphor of war is apt. We must overpower the 'enemy'. The temptation is to pick the most efficient way to attack what we see as the problem – that is what the reward structure persuades one to do.

In that sense, quarterly numbers are not just the bane of our modern-day corporations; they are in many ways the story of modernity. And this broad framework is taught in our schools and colleges; it is in the very air in which the new generation grows, reinforcing the way we think and the path humanity will take.

A conversation on the ill-effects of chemicalised farming is not very likely to hit home in India where students have been weaned on the idea that the 'green revolution', involving high-yielding grain that called for higher use of pesticides and chemical fertilisers, actually helped the nation become self-sufficient in food. Weren't we dependent for our food staples on imports earlier? How long can a nation as large as India depend on foreign supplies for its wheat and rice? We solved it with the 'green revolution', as we did later our milk shortages with the 'white revolution', by importing Jersey cows and using chemicals that force lactation in the animals. Every child can have a glass of milk now. These are easy solutions that are communicated well. They tend to stick.

We are called to action by our desire to stop the damage of an extractive economy that has given us poisons in our food chain, poisons in the air we breathe, and toxicity in our ways of working, relating and living

This, then, is the trap and the tyranny of 'development' and 'progress'. Often, we invent experiments and metrics to 'prove' that it is working. As Nassim Nicholas Taleb said: "You can disguise charlatanism under the weight of equations..." (Taleb, 2004). The approach takes us to what looks like a better place before it ends up leaving us worse off, like a child in a candy store unrestrained by the hand of a well-meaning guardian. Now, as the sugar rush brings on its inevitable problems, we are called to action by our desire to stop the damage of an extractive economy that has given us poisons in our food chain, poisons in the air we breathe, and toxicity in our ways of working, relating and living. Because we can see and measure the damage today, it is not difficult to convince an increasing number that we must change course.

Three observations can be made in this context. First, that we recognise and can measure the damage today is good. That means we are beginning to see the problem. Second, the way we seek to solve the problem is not good enough; it is even worrying. Our 'green' solutions with 'intelligent' design are often unintelligent and unwise. Third, the problem and the problem-solving interlock miss the deeper story of values that lies at the root of our troubles.

We begin with the first. There is a growing chorus for sustainable living. Today, businesses do CSR, school students are taught to care for the planet, organic food is almost a movement, and leaders of all kinds and in many fields are going 'green'. The rising tide of support from ordinary people and notably young audiences on ecological issues is clearly a good change. In the conversations in this book, we follow the eye of the everyday citizen as we ask simple questions of a monk-teacher-activist-friend-philosopher, who has had the good fortune not to be corrupted by the limited ways in which most of us have been taught in our schools and universities.

This takes us to the second point. Action on environmental issues is good, but not good enough if it is not accompanied by a cautious relook at some of the practices that brought us this destruction in the first place. While there is a lot of interest in the environment, there are equally a lot of quick fixes being delivered through the very means that caused the problem in the first place. These solutions are mostly reductionist, mechanistic and technocentric, seeking to solve complex problems with loaded, poorly understood interventionist approaches that build and seek to reorder the natural world to suit our whims. The anthropocentric 'I' is in the lead.

We try to conquer the Sars-Cov-2 pandemic with vaccines that can be developed in ever shortening time spans, only to discover that the virus mutates faster. New strains show up. We begin to realise that uprooting nature as seen in rapacious deforestation, expansionism and extractive economic institutions can increase the risk of novel diseases. Even the World Economic Forum admitted as much and said: "The pandemic is a stark reminder of our dysfunctional relationship with nature." (Quinney, 2020). We can continue to build antibiotic formulations that fight bacterial diseases, but their improper or rampant use means the bacteria, too, develop their own resistance. One horrific end result of that is drug-resistant TB, which is difficult to treat. We have genetically modified mosquitoes with an 'intelligent design' that will lead to their offspring dying before they are mature enough to bite humans and transmit disease; 750 million of them are to be released into the Florida Keys. Oxitec, a US-owned, UK-based biotech firm, has already 'deployed' these GM mosquitoes in the Cayman Islands and in Brazil. The company has an office in India too. Oxitec scientist Kevin Gorman was quoted by the *Associated Press* wire as saying: "It's gone extremely well. We have released over a billion of our mosquitoes over the years. There is no potential for risk to the environment or humans." (Anderson, 2020). Yet, in 2019, a team of independent researchers reported that some offspring of GM mosquitoes survived and produced offspring that also made it to sexual maturity, according to the magazine *Science*. It quoted one of the researchers, Jeffrey Powell of Yale University, who did the study with Brazilian researchers, as saying: "The important thing is something unanticipated happened...When people develop transgenic lines or anything to release, almost all of their information comes from laboratory studies. ...Things don't always work out the way you expect." (Servick, 2019)

These are the frontlines of growth and development. They are reinforced in many of our schools and colleges and polished up in our MBA institutes that feed the next generation of managers and leaders in business. We are led to believe we are in control. The late Sumantra Ghoshal said it well in the title of a paper in the Academy of Management Learning and Education, 'Bad Management Theories are Destroying Good Management Practices'. He wrote:

Combine agency theory with transaction cost economics, add in standard versions of game theory and negotiation analysis, and the picture of the manager that emerges is one that is now very familiar in practice: the ruthlessly hard-driving, strictly top-down, command-and-control focused, shareholder-value-obsessed, win at any cost business leader...

(Ghoshal, 2005)

What messages do these approaches and teachings send out to our people, particularly to our youth? How do you square the message of controlling, training and taming nature with Satish Kumar's voice that says killing is prohibited in his idea of good living, even the killing of a mosquito?

This brings us to the third part, which is about the values we seek to live by. The 'problem-attack-solve' linearity does not engage with the subject. It uses the desire and energy for a new order but it is anchored in the ideas of utility maximisation. In this frame, environmental degradation is one more problem that has to be 'fixed' so that production and consumption can go on unabated, even accelerated.

Very little of this is about a fundamental rewiring of humanity, a new story that seeks to relook, rethink and reconnect with the rhythms of the Earth. In the absence of this fundamental change, all other actions will be patchwork fixes, turning green into another mantra, like GDP. In fact:

It is no coincidence that the emergence of sustainability as an issue comes at a time when faith in economic progress is waning. Indeed, to declare that an action is sustainable seems today to be serving a function similar to declaring it efficient in the past. In neither case is it meant to be a precise statement about the consequences of the action.

(Nelson, 1995)

We have a new tune in town that everyone is humming but it is fundamentally repackaging a failed story. As Satish Kumar notes, a lot of the ecosystem is about "money making money", not serving the needs of society. Adam Grant, who wrote the bestseller *Give and Take,* is a successful author and professor at The Wharton School. Grant has a large fan following, including among his students, as he promotes the power of giving rather than taking. He is reported to never say 'No', and almost always engages and stretches himself to help others. He brings a refreshing and sunny side to dealing with all kinds of people. He is quite naturally loved, and he finds that the connections he creates from all this energise and empower his work. Yet, there is a manner in the giving that has a slight twist to it. The *New York Times* explains his idea and method of giving:

The most successful givers, Grant explains, are those who rate high in concern for others but also in self-interest. And they are strategic in their giving – they give to other givers and matchers, so that their work has the maximum desired effect; they are cautious about giving to takers; they give in ways that reinforce their social ties; and they consolidate their giving into chunks, so that the impact is intense enough to be gratifying. (Grant incorporates his field's findings into his own life with methodical rigor: one reason he meets with students four and a half hours in one day rather than spreading it out over the week is that a study found that consolidating giving yields more happiness).

(Dominus, 2013)

Needless to say, a movement to support people to give, help and share must be celebrated. But is giving for the sake of the joy of giving or done with an eye on the returns? Or, do we look at both? And if so, how far is that from the idea that giving can be gamed? The flourishing of giving is then rooted in the idea of taking, reducing the experience of sharing to the standard of a market-related transaction.

Contrast this approach with what the Indian saint of the sixteenth century, Goswami Tulsidas, encountered in Rahim Khane-e-Khanan, a poet who lived during the rule of the Mughal emperor Akbar. Rahim was known to offer alms, head bowed. Tulsidas asks him:

"Aisi deni den jyoon, kith sikhe ho sain, jyo jyo kar ooncho karo, tyoo tyoo neeche nain. (Oh, saintly one, where have you learnt this art of giving. Every time you give and the more you give, the more you lower your eyes)."

And Rahim replies:

"Devan haar koi aur hai, devat jyo din rain, log hamka brahm karen, taaso neeche nain. (The giver is someone else, the one who brings us the cycle of day and night; people think I am giving, and that is why I lower my eyes in shame!)" (Velishala, 2016)

Or consider what the ancient Indian texts had to say about giving. Chaturvedi Badrinath, in the book *The Mahabharata: An Inquiry in the Human Condition*, explains the message in the epic about giving and sharing – that they are more than mere rituals.

> *What is of utmost importance is the fact that the Mahabharata* gives a radically different meaning to dana, not as 'alms giving' or 'charity' as ritual acts, but sharing what one has been given, in the awareness that one's life is connected with other beings. Hospitality is an expression of that awareness, and not just 'a rule of etiquette'. If the awareness of one's human bond with others is absent in one's actual conduct, then everything one may possess is* vritha, useless ... *Through another story, the Mahabharata teaches that, 'Should one's enemy arrive at one's doorstep, one should, and with respect too, attend upon him. A tree does not withdraw its cooling shade even from one who has come to cut it.'*
>
> (Badrinath, 2013)

Gandhi's favourite song 'Vaishnava jana to' celebrates the idea of goodness and Godliness as residing in one who can understand the pain of another. The opening lines of the song, written by the fifteenth-century Gujarati poet Bhagat Narsinh Mehta, read: "A Godlike man is one who feels another's pain, who shares another's sorrow; And pride he does disdain." (Mehta, 15th Century)

These are ideas of oneness, togetherness, connectedness. They cannot be fathomed, let alone practised, in a society into which has been hammered the almost blind application of the reductionist approaches of science, the utility-maximisation goals of economics, and the promise of a happy life waiting to arrive only when growth is good and poverty is banished. Poverty has been reduced if not banished in large parts of the West, but where has it taken the people and society? Mindless consumption is the norm and is seen as *nirvana** in a world where material success masks an inner void that gathers 'loves' and 'likes' on social media for external validation. To escape this trap requires a very different kind of education and experiences from those available or provided to the vast majority. E.F. Schumacher explains how we landed here in the first place:

The loss of the vertical dimension meant that it was no longer possible to give an answer, other than a utilitarian one, to the question, 'What am I to do with my life?' The answer could be more individualistic-selfish or more social-unselfish, but it could not help being utilitarian; either 'Make yourself as comfortable as you can' or 'Work for the greatest happiness of the greatest number.' Nor was it possible to define the nature of man other than that as that of an animal... None of this leads to a helpful answer to the question, 'What am I to do with my life?'... Traditional wisdom had a reassuringly plain answer: Man's happiness is to move higher, to develop his highest faculties, to gain knowledge of the higher and highest things, and, if possible, to 'see God'.
(Schumacher, 2011)

What does this mean for a student, a manager, a consumer? The desire for change on the outside can be sustained and fuelled only when accompanied by an effort to change on the inside. This is a journey into exploring inner motivations, aspirations and hopes. Satish Kumar's conversations offer a nourishing playground for these ideas. He nudges us into the arms of Mother Earth and the wide cosmos, a good university.

A re-enchantment with nature and the wilderness is the god that can teach and evoke a sense of inquiry, humility and awe

A re-enchantment with nature and the wilderness is the god that can teach and evoke a sense of inquiry, humility and awe that is very different from what is taught in most of our schools and colleges. Henry David Thoreau speaks "of the 'spirits' of the huckleberry and of fungus as so obviously ... related to ourselves..." (Johnson, 2014)

'the humblest fungus betrays a life akin to my own.' He also recognises spirit as it pertains to forces that are not specific life forms. In Cape Cod, for instance, he acknowledges the 'spiritual ocean' and refers to a strong wind as 'Spirit's breath'. In his Journal, he declares that the

autumnal browning leaves of a shrub oak, in spite of having lost their summer green, 'still have a kind of life in them' and are 'spiritual'. On May 12, 1857, he hears the song of a 'bay-wing' and recognises 'the spirit of its earth song,' which recalls for Thoreau 'the world that we jointly inhabit'. These are clearly significant moments for Thoreau; indeed, it seems that only when he is reminded to think beyond his own corporeality and toward his interconnectedness with other forms of matter does he deem himself 'a competent witness to the world'.

(Johnson, 2014)

Experiences such as these are transformative. They mark the beginning of a journey in which one's separateness (I versus the world) gives way to the emergence of a child of the universe in communion with the air and the mountains, with the plants and the animals, and with the cosmic dance of the heavens. The observed world then is not separate from the observer. The two can merge into one sacred whole. This is the offering of ecological spirituality, a movement in which Satish Kumar is an important voice.

The approach offers a path out of the many divisions that breed violence, anxiety and tear us apart, and are an entrenched part of the global order. Donal O'Mahony, a Capuchin priest based in South Africa, writes:

The present agony of the earth should alert us to the short-sightedness of solving difficulties by seeking only to alter the outer world. Yet an ecological spirituality must of necessity make us more sensitive to social needs. Every time nature is wantonly destroyed; every time there is a situation of injustice; every time violence is used against others; every time the principle of 'relationality' is interrupted by attitudes of domination – for example, creditor countries over debtor countries, or rulers over peoples, or men over women, or humans over nature ... then those living an ecological spirituality should be quick to experience the pain and will want to do something about it. If human beings are part of the earth, then degrading the planet is diminishing part of our larger selves. Nature is not something outside us. We are something inside it.'

(O'Mahony, 2005)

The vision that can open up in this thinking is of the universe as me in action, so all actions that violate the sacredness of the universe violate me and my sacred beliefs. Put simply, it's living in harmony with the soil, the soul and society, to use the plain terminology of Satish Kumar. No punditry is required to get this right.

And that is all that is needed to begin to build a new generation of people, about the likes of whom the cab driver who took me to Schumacher College from the railway station at Totnes, said, "Oh, those people who want to change the world!"

References

Anderson, C. (2020) *Florida Keys to release modified mosquitoes to fight illness.* https://bit.ly/Satish01

Badrinath, C. (2013) *The Mahabharata: An inquiry into the human condition.* Orient BlackSwan

Dominus, S. (2013) 'The saintly way to succeed', *The New York Times Magazine*

Ghoshal, S. (2005) 'Bad management theories are destroying good management practices'. *Academy of Management Learning and Education,* 4(1), 75-91

Johnson, R. (2014) '"The only real Elysium": Thoreau's meeting of spirit and matter'. *The Thoreau Society Bulletin, Fall* (287), 6-8

Mehta, B. N. (15th Century). *Vasihnava jana to* (K. Singh, Trans.). https://bit.ly/Satish02

'Men and Women of Today'. (1929, June 29). *Dundee Courier*

Nelson, H. R. (1995) 'Sustainability, efficiency, and god: Economic values and the sustainability debate'. *Annual Review of Ecology and Systematics, 26*, 135-154.

O'Mahony, D. (2005) 'The Voice of the Earth: Towards an ecological spirituality'. *The Furrow, 56*(3), 152-159

Quinney, M. (2020) 'The COVID-19 recovery must focus on nature.' https://bit.ly/Satish03

Schumacher, E. (2011). *A Guide for the Perplexed.* Vintage

Servick, K. (2019). Study on DNA spread by genetically modified mosquitoes prompts backlash. *Science.* https://doi.org/10.1126/science.aaz5392

Taleb, N. N. (2004). *Fooled by Randomness.* Random House

Velishala, M. (2016, September 19). Tulsidas to Rahim. Message posted to https://bit.ly/Satish04

COVER 2:

A Long Walk: From being to becoming

By Sudarshan Iyengar

From the title it may appear that this is a commentary on the philosophy of being and becoming. It is not; it is about the journey of Satish Kumar, a man whose guiding stars on his journey of life were Mahatma Gandhi (1869-1948), the Indian independence leader noted for his non-violent protests against colonial rule, and Vinoba Bhave (1895-1982), who was Gandhi's associate and considered by many Gandhians as his spiritual successor. After Gandhi's death, Bhave assumed leadership of a group engaged in constructive activities suggested by Gandhi, which came to be known as the Sarvodaya movement.

Satish Kumar's distilled wisdom is contained in his formulation of 'soil-soul-society' – *prithvi, atma, samaj* – the trinity that he says underlies sustainability of humankind's existence on Earth. This wisdom flows from having lived in two worlds – in India, for the first three decades of his life, and then in England, where he has been living ever since. Thus, Satish Kumar is no armchair philosopher or academic; his experiences inform his ideas and his understanding.

Gandhi, whose full name was Mohandas Karamchand Gandhi grew from being Mohan (a name many ordinary Indians carry, and in this case short for Mohandas) to Mahatma, the great soul. His was indeed a unique journey from being to becoming. His life stages were the reverse of Satish Kumar's. Gandhi began as a householder and turned into something of a monk, though one deeply entrenched in this-worldly affairs. Babu Rajendra Prasad, the first President of India, has succinctly described this transformation in the foreword he wrote in January 1954 for the book

Mahatma Gandhi: A Life through Lenses (Publications Division, Government of India). He wrote:

> *During his life of nearly four score years, Mahatma Gandhi passed through more phases than perhaps any other man of like stature. Being born in a middle-class Vaishnava* family and brought up in that atmosphere till he joined school, and received instructions according to the system then prevailing, he lived, dressed and dined in the way all children of that class did. Later he went to England for studies and changed his dress to suit the conditions of that country. On his return to India, after being called to the bar, he passed through difficult times as all beginners in the profession of law have to and it was as a lawyer that he went to South Africa to help a client. He had, however, to spend many years there as the conditions of Indians and the treatment they received demanded that he should serve them rather than return to India. His struggle with the authorities brought about a considerable change in his life and by the time he returned to India, he had already become a sanyasi though he never put on the saffron robe of a sanyasi.*
>
> (Publications Division, 1954)

I do not intend to compare the two lives here. In fact, Satish Kumar has followed the Gandhian tenets and has wrought out of them his own 'trinity', viewing it through his prism of understanding. Gandhi did not talk about any 'trinity' explicitly. But his life and message convey to humanity that for sustained and harmonious existence, the *vyakti** [individual] has to evolve into a self-regulated entity whose quest is a search for truth through non-violence. Such an evolving person has to engage in constructive programmes in society [*samashti*]. If harmony between *vyakti* and *samashti** is established, harmony with *prakriti* [nature] is established by itself.

From monk to householder

It is rare for a nine-year-old decide to become a monk. Satish Kumar was an exception. He was determined. The old Brahmin tutor who used to come to his home to teach the children was very angry when he came to know about the boy's wish. He shouted at Satish Kumar's mother: "In your old age you have lost all sense ... He is not destined to be a monk. I know his horoscope and I know his stars. I tell you that he cannot stay a monk, so stop him now." (Kumar, 1992)

A Jain monk's life is perhaps the toughest. When he was taken into the order his head was shaved, and a tuft of hair which was left behind was plucked out by the guru in a ritual of initiation. Now, as a novice monk, Satish Kumar was not allowed to brush his teeth, to bathe, to change clothes or to cut his hair. Fleas appeared on his scalp and, when they fell out when he scratched his head, he was asked to put them back, as a Jain monk is not supposed to harm any living creature. The hair that was plucked out of his head was wrapped around his leg and knotted tight so that the fleas could have their food from his body until they died. He was then sent out to beg food from households. He went through vigorous and rigorous training in the Jain scriptures. Those lessons have stayed with him throughout his life. He witnessed *santhara* – voluntary embrace of death – by his immediate mentor, Kundan. Kundan died after completing 23 days of fasting. The child in Satish Kumar was not dead yet. He told Kundan to go to heaven and come back to tell him how wonderful it was!

Travelling with a group of monks from his order on one occasion, Satish, who was then a teenager, went down with severe malaria when they reached Jaipur. In his acute suffering, the adolescent could only think that he was being punished because of his *karma*, and maybe also because of his aberrant behaviour in having had sex, breaking the vow of celibacy he had taken. The teenager had been seduced and molested by a fellow monk. This incident had produced anger and shame. There is a striking parallel in how both Gandhi and Satish Kumar, as adolescents with strong personal morality, attributed their miseries to their carnal desires and sexual activity. Gandhi, having been in the service of his ailing father for some time, could not resist sex with his teenaged wife on the night his father died. He wrote that he felt deeply ashamed and miserable about it; he felt his animal passion had blinded him. For Satish Kumar, this way of thinking passed. But for Gandhi, the incident was a blot he was never able to efface or forget.

One of the lay disciples in the order, who acted as a guide and stayed with the group all the time, always carried a stick with a sword inside it. He considered it his duty to protect the monks from any outside trouble. How could an order that believed in strict non-violence allow something like this, was the question in the mind of young Satish. But the guru was of the view that since the guide was not a monk and lived in a world of compromise, he could carry an instrument of violence, whereas monks did not carry one! The guide's explanation was that anything could happen in the big city and how could he not protect them from evil? If he did not protect them, how could the monks live their non-violent lives?

Also, the monks did not produce their own food; neither did they cook their own food as there was violence in that activity. Some of their supporters had to do these tasks so that the monks could live a life of non-violence! Doubts and questions cropped up in young Satish Kumar's mind. Was he any closer to *moksha** (liberation from the cycle of birth and death, as understood in Indian philosophy and religion) living in this way? In Jaipur he was confronted with the contradiction of living the non-violent life under the protection of a person who was ready to practise violence to protect non-violent monks. He could sense hypocrisy in this arrangement.

Another turning point

It was with these confusions swirling in his mind that Satish went with his guru to Delhi, where he met Vinoba Bhave. He has described the first meeting:

> *Here, my guru and Vinoba met. They, the two saints, were sitting on the ground on blankets, facing each other. A hundred monks and lay disciples were gathered around them. I was sitting by my guru. I looked closely at Vinoba. He had a long white beard and no teeth; his face was scholarly and wise, his eyes half closed and peaceful. I saw this man wearing less clothes than me, but unlike me not claiming to be superior in any way – a man without a label. My guru asked me stand up and briefly explain the fundamentals of the Jain religion in Sanskrit. I recited a passage from scripture and spoke in Sanskrit. As I was talking, Vinoba looked at me and I at him. He smiled. I was touched.*

> (Kumar, 1992)

Satish Kumar wanted to be a person without a label, as you will read in his conversation with us. It is clear that Vinoba Bhave had inspired him to become the 'self', without any label.

Satish and another member of the order wanted to launch themselves independently. They begged permission for it and got it. A third companion was provided to them, and they were asked to walk to a town called Ratangarh in the north-western Indian state of Rajasthan, traversing villages where there were no disciples of the order. It took them six months to reach Ratangarh. There they settled down to the monk's routine. One day a lay disciple, Kishore, gave Satish a book written by Gandhi and insisted that he read it. As a monk, Satish was not allowed to read any non-religious book. But upon the disciple's insistence, he read the book. And this was what he understood from it:

> What Gandhi was saying was that religion is not religion if it does not help to solve the problems of this world, here and now. If a religion takes a person away from this life and this society, then it is escapism. The search for truth is a continuous daily experience. There is absolute and ultimate truth and the search for truth never ends. Every person's life is a kind of laboratory and every person should experiment with truth.
>
> (Kumar, 1992)

He and his two fellow monks discussed all this and decided to desert the order, leaving it one cold night. This was when Satish Kumar began his own experiments with truth, embarking on his journey from being a monk to becoming a soul-searching, this-worldly person. Kishore, the lay disciple who introduced Satish to Gandhi, had told them about Bodhgaya* in Bihar, the place where the Buddha attained enlightenment, where a Jain monk had become a *sadhak* [*one who follows a given practice as a disciple*] and worked in Vinoba's *bhoodan** movement under which land owners were encouraged to give away a part of their land to landless peasants. *Bhoodan* was a new coinage and a powerful social experiment. The word itself was formed by the merger of two Hindi words, *bhoo*, meaning land, and *dan* meaning alms or charity so that *bhoodan* literally meant the giving away of land. Satish Kumar decided to go there and begin his new life.

Satish was a child when he joined the order and left it as a youth of 19. It is difficult to gauge from his own account whether he had a strong intuitive feeling about the spiritual urge within him. However, having been a monk as a child and a teenager, Satish had had a different type of schooling from other children. He was schooled in religious studies, where memorising was the main method of learning. What he memorised he had to eventually share with lay people in a learned manner. He was a bright student, as is evident from his guru choosing him to demonstrate his knowledge to Vinoba. But the young Satish Kumar was disillusioned quickly by the ways of the order, and he dared to leave. The pronouncement of the Brahmin teacher years ago to his mother turned out to be prophetic! Satish Kumar's life journey for the next 12 years involved a lot of travelling ... in search of what his inner self longed for. Exactly what that was, he himself was not sure about.

The principles and values of Gandhi and Vinoba appealed to Satish. Youth also brought its own pleasures and pains. When at Bodhgaya, where he lived for a year in the ashram, he was sent to Gaya town, where he learned the craft of spinning on the *ambar** [a modern version of the traditional spinning wheel that was a tool and a symbol of the Indian independence movement] and also had his first encounter with a *kothewali** [traditionally a singer and entertainer who also selectively provided sex services]. After a year at the ashram, he was sent to a nearby village to work in the fields. This was his first exposure to working with the soil. He toiled happily, and perhaps this began his association with the soil, which became central to his philosophical concerns later in life. He developed an infatuation for a girl who worked with him. He expressed his feelings to her and even proposed marriage. But the girl was from a lower caste* of untouchables*, and her father declined his offer as he did not want to break the caste boundaries that helped him live harmoniously within the society by not challenging its discriminations.

This was a lesson for Satish. He had thought he was being revolutionary in following the path of Gandhi and Vinoba, who worked to break the caste system's stranglehold on Indian society. But the social systems prevailing in Indian society were so rigid on both sides that none would dare to break them. Even today, many parts of India, especially Gujarat, Haryana, Uttar Pradesh and Bihar, continue to witness 'honour killings' over inter-caste marriage. Continued rigid social hierarchical structures can defeat all reformist laws and institutions. The caste arithmetic continues to play an important part in India's electoral politics to this day.

Satish left the village to join Vinoba's *padayatra**, a journey by foot, for *bhoodan*. Walking with Vinoba was an opportunity to learn directly from the master his concepts of non-violence, civil disobedience and *satyagraha*. Walking was no strain for Satish; he was trained and seasoned in it during his years as a monk. In the course of the *padayatra,* the young Satish was again attracted to a beautiful young woman. But when he proposed marriage to her, the lady declined. She suggested that their relationship remain platonic. Both had come to stay in Khadigram ashram, which was noted for its Gandhian activities and located in Bodhgaya, Buddhism's holiest shrine because it is the place where the Buddha attained enlightenment The ashram head warned them against their growing intimacy. Satish soon left the place and moved to Benares, or Varanasi, a city on the Ganges river in India's most populous state, Uttar Pradesh. It was essential now that he earn his living, so he joined *Sarvodaya* magazine as a deputy editor. He learned the skills of editing, proofreading, publishing and printing. The editor, a well-known Sarvodaya leader, Siddhraj Daddha, found him an eligible bachelor and advised that he become a householder. He suggested a match too.

How could one be happy? Not by chasing one's own happiness, but by loving someone else and by making someone else happy.

Satish Kumar had gone through a unique experience in Benares before he got married. He used to visit a Nepalese Shiva temple. The walls of the temple were covered with erotic sculptures and carvings of gods and goddesses in various postures of union. At the centre of the temple was a large *Shiva Lingam* [a representation of Shiva in the form of a stylised penis], erect, penetrating the *yoni* [vagina] of Parvati, the goddess. The keeper of the temple, Babaji, was a yogi. Curious about what he saw, Satish asked Babaji what the connection between sexual union and spiritual experience was. Babaji explained to him that the way of *tantra** was the way of sacred sex. How could one be happy? Not by chasing one's own happiness, but by loving someone else and by making someone else happy. That was the paradox. When one loses oneself, one finds the self. When a man and a woman were united in their bodies, they were free of all physical and mental tension. There was no contradiction or dichotomy between sensuality, sexuality and spirituality. Babaji's explanation left a deep impression on Satish Kumar's mind. He had longed for such a union for years. He had assumed that he would experience it with his wife when they consummated their marriage, but that experience was disastrous. The act happened, but he failed to experience any bliss. It was no sublime union, and the passion he was so eagerly anticipating never came to bloom. Satish Kumar's quest for union of his soul with the Supreme continued. For the present, though, he was entrenched in worldly affairs.

Speaking the truth reflects fearlessness in a person. Gandhi called this *abhaya*. It was one of 11 vows that Gandhians were asked to take and practise. At the Khadigram ashram, the inmates chanted the *ekadash vrat* (The eleventh day of both the waxing and waning moon is called *ekadash*.

Vrat could mean vow or fasting. The eleven prescribed vows were: *satya* [truth], *ahimsa* [non-violence, love], *brahmacharya* [chastity], *aswada* [control of the palate], *asteya* [non-stealing], *aparigraha** [non-possession or voluntary poverty], *abhaya* [fearlessness], removal of untouchability*, bread labour, equality of religions & tolerance and *swadeshi* [use of locally produced goods] scripted by Gandhi. He had made it one of the ashram's observances.

Satish had to often pay the price for speaking the truth as he perceived it. In Benares, a new Gandhian building complex costing about half a million rupees was being constructed. It included the offices of the paper where he was a deputy editor. Satish and a few others were of the opinion that the structure "could not be considered an example of simple living of the Gandhian kind" (Kumar, 1992). He wrote an article in a local newspaper criticising the financing of such an expensive structure from the donation money, which could have been used for work in the villages. He also criticised the establishment of an academic institution, Gandhian Institute of Studies, for which the plans were to employ high-salaried university graduates producing research on paper. The deputy director of the institute did not take kindly to Satish Kumar's newspaper article and sacked the young man. Satish held that such structures and institutions as wings of the Gandhian establishment were "career-conscious, western-suited, city-oriented, intellectual, salary-seeking – those who felt it necessary to do a public relations job on the movement to fit it to the urban, industrial twentieth century"(Kumar, 1992). This has proved to be the reality even in the present twenty-first century!

Satish's quest for nourishment of the soul and his search for the meaning of life continued. A disciple of Vinoba's, known as Swamiji, had set up an ashram in the Nilgiri hills near Bengaluru, the capital city of the Southern Indian State of Karnataka, and was looking for people to work there. The jobless Satish Kumar found this an exciting offer. His wife too was happy at the prospect. They moved.

Walking for world peace

September 11, 2001, or 9/11, has come to be recognised as a historic day because of the deadly terrorist attack on the twin towers of the World Trade Centre in New York, a symbol of the prosperous and pompous neo-liberal world. It led to counter-violence by America, which the 'rational' world justified. Peace initiatives the world over suffered a serious setback as a result. An event on the same day in September forty years earlier in 1961 occurred in Trafalgar Square, London, and in Holy Loch in Scotland, where Bertrand Russell and his 1,600 young colleagues raised their voice and took to non-violent civil disobedience against the nuclear armament race between the superpowers of the day, the USA and the erstwhile USSR. This was a major peace initiative that caught world attention. Russell was arrested and jailed for seven days in Brixton prison. Thousands of miles away in Bengaluru in India, a news item about this in an English local newspaper caught the attention of E.P. Menon, a young man dedicated to the Gandhi-Vinoba path. It gripped his imagination. He saw it as a call to the conscience of humanity from an 89-year-old man in prison. He also learned that a group of young people had planned a peace march from Washington to Moscow. This inspired Menon, and he resolved to walk from Moscow to Washington. He started looking for a companion.

After contacting a few people he knew, he approached Satish Kumar, whom he had met in 1956 when Menon had worked in Gaya. And Satish Kumar's life as a walking pilgrim began once again.

One is reminded of the *shlokas** from the *Aiteraya Brahmana**, Volume 3, Chapter 3, which convey a profound message as to how to live life. In brief, the message is, *charaiveti, charaiveti** – literally, 'keep walking'. Satish has been walking all his life, crossing from stage to stage. Currently, he is in the fourth stage of his life. And the *shloka* for this stage is as follows:

कलिः शयानो भवति संजिहानस्तु द्वापरः ।
उत्तिष्ठस्त्रेता भवति कृतं संपाद्यते चरंश्चरैवेति ॥

Loosely translated, the *shloka* means:

Sleep is '*kali-yuga*', waking up is '*dwapar yuga*'
Standing up is '*treta yuga*', but only the one who endeavours reaches '*satya yuga*', Hence, keep working, keep walking.

In Hindu cosmology, *yugas** are understood to mean various ages through the journey of humankind with progressively declining moral standards, beginning from the age of truth called *satya yuga* and ending in *kali yuga* with its low standards, the age we are supposed to be in now.

In his autobiography, Satish Kumar does not analyse his gains and lessons from his global walk. Yet, crisscrossing the globe on foot cannot but bring huge learnings as there is considerable interface with nature, life forms, humanity and civilisations. It is known as *deshatan** [a journey to gather experiences] in Sanskrit. Every youth was to take it up for a year after completing his education in a *gurukul** [a traditional residential schooling system] to familiarise himself with worldly affairs before entering the world and becoming a family man or a *grihastha**. The monk Satish Kumar had done *deshatan* within the country, and now it was a *deshatan* of the globe, carrying a message for world peace.

Charaiveti, charaiveti*

Satish's *gristhashram* or family living in India did not work well after his worldwide recognition, appreciation and jubilant return. He wanted to read, write, share and learn. He could not perform the duties expected of a normal householder, which in his case was to run a curtain shop – a business of his in-laws. When Satish refused to sit at the shop, a stiff argument with his wife followed, after which she left for her maternal home with their two children. A friend from Delhi came to help Satish out of his desolation. The friend offered him work as a deputy editor for a magazine he was editing and publishing in Delhi. Satish moved to Delhi from Benares and tried to give his best. But the magazine did not do well, leaving him still unsettled and restless.

A letter from the Italian Danilo Dolci (1924-1997), who later came to be known as the Gandhi of Sicily, inviting him to join a march from Naples to Rome for peace, beckoned. The letter was "like a raft to a drowning man" (Kumar, 1992) for Satish. He shared it with his friend from Benares and both left for the peace march in Italy. The pilgrim had again set out on his quest for truth and for care of his soul. About leaving Delhi for the march, Satish Kumar notes that he just walked out, leaving everything – magazine, office, papers, flat, furniture – to die without him.

After the Naples-Rome peace march, he floated about for a while, wandering in Europe. During this period, he went through an ecstatic experience of bodily union with an artist, which he had not experienced even in his conjugal life. He felt this must be the bliss which the yogi *pujari* (priest) of the Nepalese Shiva temple in Benares had told him about. When he was in Prague, he met Canon John Collins, a British champion of the African liberation struggle, whom he joined in setting up an institution, the 'London School of Non-Violence'. It was the Gandhi centenary year, and what better way to pay his tribute to his guiding star? They conducted workshops, exhibitions and training programmes. But the pilgrim's restlessness showed no signs of ebbing. London was crowded, full of smoke and manifest consumerism. He missed India and its people. Collins agreed to pay his air fare to Delhi. Satish instead suggested that Collins gift him a used car. He drove to Delhi and arrived on 2 October 1969. *Charaiveti, charaiveti.*

Here, Vinoba's land reform movement beckoned again. Satish went to Chatturpur village in Saharsa district of Bihar. It was a time India was witness to the movement of non-violence and the rise of a counter movement that stood for an armed rebellion. On the one hand there was Vinoba Bhave with his inspiring idea of *bhoodan** which later turned to making entire villages with collective ownership of land, the so-called *gramdani** village. On the other hand, Satish Kumar's close friend had become a Naxalite, a member of a violent movement named for the local area called Naxalbari in West Bengal State, where an armed uprising by far-Left radical communists was launched in 1967. Naxalites believed that the oppressed had to be awakened, mobilised and organised for fighting for their property rights on the lands they tilled. Violence was their way to get land for themselves from the landlords. They believed that non-violent methods and *karuna** [kindness or softness] would not solve their problems and that *katla** [violence, literally beheading] was the only way left.

Chatturpur was a *gramdani* village where all land had been turned to collective ownership under the *bhoodan* movement. Vinoba wanted to protest against the violent ways of the comrades, but legal reforms were painfully slow. So he said that it was not through killing – *katla* – and not through the law – *kanoon* – but through compassion – *karuna* – that he would ask for land. The enthusiasm had reached new heights in Bihar. The *bhoodan* workers impressed upon Vinoba that each and every village in Bihar had become a *gramdani* village, where private land became collectively-owned land. The reality on the ground was very different, and was seen in the rise of the Naxalites.

On his way to Chatturpur village, Satish Kumar had an encounter with a Naxalite youth who warned him to go away saying *gramdani* workers only delayed the revolution. In the village, the oppressed classes reported that a long time ago, Vinoba's people had visited and promised them land; then came the communists promising them land; and then the government officers, also promising land, but nothing had moved. Lately, there was a youth from their caste who had been saying that none would give them land and they would have to take it by killing the landlords. The landlords had threatened to destroy the share croppers' settlements and evict them. Satish Kumar could sense that Vinoba's slogan '*katla se nahi, kanoon se nahi par karuna se'* (not by killing, not by the law but with compassion) had not succeeded. He realised the agony of the untouchables* in their struggle to be part of a *gramdani* village. He left dejected.

> *I saw the events of my life as one thread, the same thread which united the whole universe and which was each person.*

Satish Kumar's pilgrimage continued for another year in the form of his stay on a farm in the forests around the Vindhya mountains in a village named Jumudi in Uttar Pradesh State. He toiled in the fields and roamed the forests. Caring for the soul and soil continued. A sudden realisation occurred one day when he sat down under a tree and went into meditation:

> *One morning, I got up early and walked into the forest. It was dawn ... I came to a tall tree with large overhanging branches, sat down cross-legged under the tree and closed my eyes. I looked into my body and saw a dark tunnel, a deep hollow inside; I went into it, drawn inwards.*
>
> *Instead of smelling outside, my nose was smelling the inner happenings and my ears were hearing the sounds inside. I could hear the sounds and voices of the ego pushing me in different directions. But I sat quietly. Slowly the battle calmed down, it slowly faded away. Gradually peace came.*
>
> *I saw the events of my life as one thread, the same thread which united the whole universe and which was each person. I saw a struggle without conflict, a pain without misery. I saw a love so great that it had to remain hidden ... I was being reborn ... engaged in the journey from action to non-action, from struggle without to struggle within. Life was an eternal journey, a journey to the centre, the source, searching for the soul.*
>
> *...I felt a sense of divinity. This newness brought a surrender, where nothing mattered, where everything was accepted. I was beyond happiness, beyond pleasure. I experienced the zero level of existence, the void, the beauty of the void and the beauty of nothingness – shunyata.*
>
> (Kumar, 1992)

Satish Kumar had come to an important milestone in his spiritual quest. He realised how to care for the soul.

Caring for soil and society

The revolution in East Pakistan in 1971 leading to the formation of a new nation called Bangladesh saw Satish following the path of *charaiveti charaiveti** again. He went to London at the invitation of his friend John Collins with exhibition material illustrating the situation in Bangladesh. At the exhibition, he met his soul partner. Intriguingly, a yogi astrologer he met at the weekly market near the forest village of Jumudi, where Satish Kumar had lived and worked on a farm, without any provocation or question from him, had told him that the wife of his friend on whose farm he lived did not like his presence; he predicted that Satish would soon travel overseas and he would meet a person who would change his life completely. After the Brahmin teacher's prediction early on in life that he would leave the monastic order, here, after 27 years, an unknown yogi was making another prediction about him that would come true.

Satish's quest for inner peace had been partially resolved. He had arrived at inner composure and peace. He had grown beyond any identity label. One part of the search was perhaps over. The distilled wisdom of this experience was recorded by him years later in his book *Soil, Soul and Society*:

> ...the individual soul is atman, the intimate being, *and the word for universal soul, or* anima mundi, *is* paramatman*, the ultimate being... In Arabic we find a similar formulation – the individual person is called khud and the divine being is khuda – just by adding an 'a', the individual is released from his or her narrow identity or ego and is transformed into divine consciousness.*
>
> *Often we are weighed down by the burden of our narrow identities of nationality, race, religion, class, gender and similar other divisive concepts and mental constructs. We become imprisoned in the idea of 'I' separate from the 'other' and 'mine' separate from the 'other's'. Through universal love we are able to break out of this ego and become part of the eco – making a quantum leap by changing from 'g' to 'c'.*
>
> (Kumar, 2013)

As a monk, Satish Kumar had read, memorised, chanted verses and given sermons about the necessity of one's release from one's narrow identity of the self to become one with the ultimate being, which he understood as *moksha**. But his own realisation came when he became a *grihastha**, *a householder,* and had interface with society.

The seed of the idea of care for soil was planted in his mind perhaps when he went in search of Vinoba's way of caring for soil and society. Engaging in working with the hands by spinning yarn and digging the soil to make it productive for farming, Satish may have begun to realise the need to care for the earth. Between his pilgrimages for peace, he always came back to care for the soil, in the literal sense. His last attempt in India at this was when he tried to be Vinoba's *gramdani* worker on a farm belonging his friend's father. He was disillusioned with the work itself, but that was where he had his inner self-realisation.

Meeting his soulmate did transform his life. As did parenting a child and accepting the editorship of the periodical *Resurgence,* nurturing soul and society. He began reading the works of original and wonderful thinkers who had deep insights about soil, soul and society. His concern and longing for the soil continued, until the family decided to move to rural England and began natural farming and tending animals. His connection with soil was immediate and deep. He realised the connection, and out of this evolved the formulation of his trinity of soil, soul and society.

The pilgrim in Satish never disappeared, even after he settled down to the life of a *grihastha,* tilling the soil, tending animals, editing *Resurgence,* and running a school on principles similar to Gandhi's concept of *Nai Talim**. The term was coined in a national education conference in Wardha in 1937, presided over by Gandhi who offered his concept of *Nai Talim* or *Buniyadi Talim* – basic education – at the time. It involves education of the heart (through living and working together while learning), of the hands (education based on a vocation as the base to skill oneself), and of the head (gaining knowledge). In 1985, when he turned 50, the age *grihastha ashram* ends in the Hindu way of life, he decided to go on a pilgrimage again. The *charaiveti charaiveti* lesson remained in him. It was a *padayatra**. It was as a non-Christian outsider on a pilgrimage to the holy places of Britain. It was not only a spiritual journey for him but he gained a lot of learning from the people he met. A bishop told him that silence was the casualty of gadgetry. A family told him it was difficult for them to believe how Christians had embraced the industrial society. His understanding of the trinity of soil, soul and society deepened on the pilgrimage. He said:

Pilgrimage is, among other things, a spiritual form of tourism, whereas tourism has become a secular form of pilgrimage. When we journey as pilgrim, we go with a sense of sacred, without making demands – and indeed, we expect a certain amount of inconvenience and hardship on the journey, whereas secular tourism expects the world to be arranged for it. In the age of ecology, perhaps pilgrimage and tourism need to come closer together.

(Kumar, 2013)

His pilgrimages did not end with that tour in England. His soul had to experience nature (soil) in its pristine existence. In 1997, he again walked seven days from a base camp with a team of nine to Kailas Mansarovar. According to him, Mount Kailas was mysterious, majestic and monumental. No words could describe the experience of being there, at the towering temple of nature. It was magical camping there.

Chara eva – to keep walking – did not stop for Satish Kumar, who sees 'no destination' to get to. The walk continues for the soul that is in the body and lives with soil and society. His key to his way of finding the trinity is *charaiveti charaiveti.*

The wisdom underlying soil-soul-society

As a Jain monk, Satish imbibed the principles of non-violence, self-restraint and self-discipline. His was a quest for self-realisation, for *nirvana** or *moksha**. But, as he journeyed through many cultures – through Buddhism, through a deep study of the Bhagavad Gita*, one of the best known Hindu texts, he realised that the Jain principles he had imbibed for the inner self also enhanced his relationship with nature, *prakriti,* and with the social world. If human civilisation followed the principles he had imbibed, it had the potential to avoid ecological calamities, personal alienation and social injustice.

Beginning the practice of self-discipline is the beginning of *tapas**, or penance, says the Bhagavad Gita. This practice is called *tapasya,* the discipline of undergoing penance. A sadhu or a monk does it in isolation or by living in an order. Gandhi showed Satish that it can and should be done living in the world as a *grihastha.* Man is very much a part of nature, so man should in turn give to nature, which the Bhagavad Gita calls *yagna.* The third dimension to the practice is *dana* – action for the benefit of others. Gandhi's life and work guided Satish Kumar to understand his duty to perform *tapas, yagna* and *dana*. Satish delivers the same message to humanity in the trinity he advances, of soil, soul and society.

In explaining his trinity, he puts the soil first. He says all life is sustained by nature. Everything comes from the soil and returns to the soil. The fifteenth-century saint-poet Kabir wrote:

माटी कहे कुम्हार से, तू क्या रोंदे मोहे,
एक दिन ऐसा आएगा, मैं रोंदूगी तोहे ।

[The earth (soil/clay) tells the potter: you think you are kneading me, but there will come a day when I will be kneading you!]

Satish reminds us that this vital truth is forgotten. In the past few centuries, with the capacities of their head and hands, humans have 'developed' the physical world so much that an arrogant world view has emerged and has come to stay. It has changed what was our reciprocal, reverential and spiritual relationship to nature, to one of owning, commanding and manipulating nature for our own material advantage. Fritjof Capra has captured this in his reference to Francis Bacon. He notes:

> *The terms in which Bacon advocated his new empirical method of investigation were not only passionate but often outright vicious. Nature, in his view, had to be 'bounded in her wanderings,' 'bound into service,' and made a 'slave'. She was to be 'put in constraint,' and the aim of the scientist was to 'torture nature's secret from her'.*
>
> (Capra, 1983)

How does one perform *yagna*? Satish practises this by doing organic farming. This is his *yagna* - caring for the soil. According to him, one practises *yagna* by celebrating the beauty of nature.

> *If we take five trees to build our home, we must replenish them by planting 50 trees. If we have taken goodness out of the soil through crops of wheat, rice and vegetables, we must replenish the soil with manure and compost as well as leave the land fallow after seven years of cultivation, thus offering the land a sabbatical. This is what we refer to as yagna: replenishment, restoration and renewal.*
>
> (Kumar, 2013)

Satish Kumar's central message about soil is that one needs to have a deep experience of nature to be a believer in Arne Næss's 'Deep Ecology'.

Care for the soul comes next. This concept and practice is more deeply rooted in the oriental world than in other cultures. Some people in the West are certainly deeply concerned about ecological degradation, but Satish suggests that the contemporary environmental movement follows the path of empirical science, rational thinking and external action, and that humanity should include care of the soul, i.e., do *tapas*. He writes:

> *Sometimes we become convinced that the world needs saving so urgently that we force ourselves to work day in and day out to save the planet. We join environmental or peace organisations. We go on protest marches. We work harder and harder for conservation of nature. As a consequence, we neglect our wellbeing and suffer from burnout, depression, breakdown of marriage and disillusionment.*
>
> (Kumar, 2013)

This is separating soul from soil. It should not be done. *Tapas* – caring for the soul – is necessary, and inseparable from *yagna* – caring for the soil. Gandhi advocated it strongly.

Humanity in its arrogance and ignorance is not only at war with nature, it is at war with itself. Concentration of power in the economic and political arena due to our unbridled greed and ambition has disrobed every society of peace. Satish Kumar explains the basis on which care for society becomes indispensable, why it is an integral part of his trinity. He quotes from Vinoba's *Talks on Gita*. Vinoba says, "...because we are already highly obliged to society. We were totally defenceless and weak when we were born. It is society that looked after us and brought us up, we should therefore serve it."

Serving or caring for society is *dana*. This is done through *karma yoga**. Satish Kumar says a *karma yogi* or an activist should not seek any benefit from his or her own action. Rather, he or she should offer their action for the benefit of others. Gandhiji emphasised relentless improvement of the self towards becoming a self-regulated *vyakti** [individual]; he lived this. He undertook social action, *satyagraha* [non-violent resistance], and constructive programmes with *gram swarajya** [local self-government at the village level] as the main goal for society – the *samashti**. It is implied in his type of evolution of the *vyakti* and *samashti* that harmony in *srishti* – the universe – will result.

References

Capra, F. (1983). *The Turning Point*. Flamingo, UK.

Govt. of India. Ministry of Information and Broadcasting. (1954). *Mahatma Gandhi: A Life Through Lenses*. https://bit.ly/Satish05

Kumar, S. (1992). *No Destination: Autobiography of a Pilgrim*. Green Books, UK.

Kumar, S. (2013). *Soil, Soul, Society: A new trinity for our time*. Leaping Hare Press, Brighton, UK.

Servick, K. (2019). Study on DNA spread by genetically modified mosquitoes prompts backlash. *Science*. https://bit.ly/Satish06

COVER 3:

Earth is a Community

By Lisa Pearson

2015: Schumacher College

Whilst visiting the Institut du Monde Arabe, my interest had been drawn to a magazine article about the Kogi people and a feature about Satish Kumar. Satish talked about Schumacher College, Dartington, Devon and its philosophy of caring for the natural environment and each other. The college is part of the new attempt to seriously rethink our participation on Earth. With the chance to learn about polyculture, alley cropping and agroforestry, I joined the sustainable horticulture apprenticeship at the college in 2015. On reflection, one major reason for this was my anguish at finding local agricultural fields devoid of clearly visible wildlife. Monotonous, perfectly shaped monoculture. The fields are vast due to increased intensification and mechanisation. But all is far from perfect. When actively searching for a variety of birds, it was astonishing to find them not in the fields but at a landfill site. When seeking to learn the practical craft of horticulture and growing, without exploitation and using up finite resources, I needed to find an approach that did not use agrichemicals. Schumacher College stood out like a beacon because of this.

The first month at college coincided with the completion of the Holistic Science course. As we hugged goodbye, a tearful student, who had coincidentally worked with the Kogi people, said in passing that magic will happen. At college we worked with the land, learnt how to create healthy soil, sang and laughed many times. There is a real joy in embracing and connecting with nature. This means whilst trying to restore the balance of nature, we find personal balance too. There is space to be grateful. To have time to just be. To sleep under the redwoods and sense the owl swooping over. To watch with pleasure the sunrise, the sunset and the stars. To understand the rhythms of beings, including treecreepers, the elephant hawk moth, the swarming of the bees, the muntjac deer and the elusive badger within a place of beauty. When we were quiet, we heard and noticed more. We noticed the presence of plants growing in the stone walls and indicative of good air quality. There were dramatic moments such as when an Indian runner duck was killed by another animal. Then we had the chance to rear and care for ducklings. We experimented with different techniques and actively sought out what was happening in the local community; observing and taking part in the different methods of growing that promoted biodiversity, the local people and livelihood. Some were using a gift economy to sustain a simple livelihood, others worked for a Community Supported Agriculture model using minimal tillage or a forest garden.

Service at Schumacher College included helping to prepare and cook vegetarian recipes from the produce grown in the gardens, looking after the animals and composting. The kitchen and compost toilet 'wastes' were used in the composting process. Every Friday morning was our turn to wake up early and feed the ducks and chickens. This was also the time that Satish would visit and lead the meditation. I recall bursting into the college to see that Satish was ready to start, looking down at my feet, and running back red faced to take off shoes that were thickly caked in mud. Satish said "Why not meditate whilst feeding the chickens?" No need to rush, simple. Slowing down is important to learn. Learning took place in practice (or in nature) as well as in the classroom. A typical day consisted of a reading at breakfast of Pope Francis's *Laudato si*; then a tutorial on the living organisms within a handful of soil, ending with an evening talk about food sovereignty. The fireside chats led by Satish and the talented guest speakers throughout the seasons produced powerful, rich dialogue that infiltrated our college discussions. Art, craft, music and dance were integral to its fabric. Living in community also has its challenges but it is important to 'sit in the fire' with people who have opposing views. Many students from different countries felt comfortable to share their problems. They were deeply disturbed at the intensity of the current industrial economic growth at all costs, the environmental damage being caused and also the increasing inequality in their countries. Many pointed out the vacuousness of having endless material possessions alongside social media flaunting and posturing. They overwhelmingly had a deep love and concern for the natural world and concern for their people. They have moved on to make remarkable changes to their lives and the lives of others. They walk softly on this planet and with their livelihood. The circular economy is not only studied but put into practice. This confirms that the college was not named in vain. As E.F. Schumacher said: "Non-renewable goods must only be used if they are indispensable, and then only with the greatest care and the most meticulous concern for conservation."

Schumacher College is a place for celebrating and falling in love with life. Yet, like all of us, it is not without its faults. One day a group of disgruntled students pointed out sustainable changes that could be made to its infrastructure. Satish was sharp and forceful; he said: "Forget about Schumacher College, it's what you do when you leave which is important." When it became painful for me to be away from family, Satish listened to my heart and, with gentleness and sincerity, offered advice. It was also reassuring to find someone to share deeper spiritual experiences. He has undoubtedly touched and guided the lives of many people and communities. His service to the Earth and all living things is his grace.

2016-2017: Walk the talk

It was a pleasure to walk with Satish and people from around the world in 2016. He led a short pilgrimage to Oxford along the river as part of celebrations to mark 50 years of *Resurgence* magazine. Personally, this pilgrimage was about the river, reverence for the water. It was also about unity. Half way through the pilgrimage, we all lit a candle and said that it was better to light a candle than to curse the darkness. Reminiscing about Alexander Pope's 18th-century satire where the 'silver Thames' was at that time increasingly polluted and overfished, it was pleasing that this part of the meandering river appeared to be looked after and the fish were lively. On the last leg of the walk with an 'Economics for Transition' student from China, who had just completed the course at Schumacher College, we decided to take a short rest. We sat at the edge of the river bank and respectfully watched a swan who was also studying us as we dipped our sore toes gingerly in the cool water. Satish came to join us and he said he didn't mind sitting on a stinging nettle patch; he just found his cloth and sat right on top. Whilst sitting with his trousers rolled up and his feet in the water, he pondered: "Isn't it funny how the West calls this river Father Thames and we in the East call the river Mother?" This observation shows how throughout time we acknowledge from whatever country we live in that water looks after us, like a parent, so we must look after water in return. Satish taught us en route about protecting and respecting all the elements (earth, air, fire, water).

We arrived in Oxford on International World Peace Day. Part of a promotion following this walk included a black and white photograph of Satish and E.P. Menon together when they took part in their much longer peace pilgrimage around the globe. This is where the inspiration began and my imagination fired up. I had met Jagdish Rattanani at Schumacher College and this chance meeting in 2015 progressed to many discussions and ideas. Jagdish was interested in interviewing Satish, so that his wisdom and life story could be absorbed by young audiences worldwide. Introductions were made and accepted and they happily met and collaborated at Bija Vidyapeeth (Earth University) Navdanya learning centre in 2017.

2018-2020: Listen to children and Mother Earth

In my neighbourhood, a small group of primary school children initiated a discussion with concern, motivation and energy about wanting to do something to help the planet. They are hungry for information and are questioning why coral reefs and many other animals are dying. How come every river in England is polluted? They want information about what is happening and how to solve or adapt to such urgent problems. They want to know how they can respect this Earth and restore the health of the planet. It is not caring to shield them from this and carry on with the old story at such a time of flux. Why not enhance and adapt education to include eco-literacy so that our children can adapt too? They can handle the truth as they freely share their sadness and loss with each other and look up to their elders for possible direction and information. It would be healthier to allow space as a group to listen to this expression of hurt, vulnerability, fragility and uncertainty.

People in the UK are starting to reduce their meat intake, whether to stop the juggernaut of the meat and dairy industry or in response to the degradation of the land and pollution of the air and water courses. Global consumption pushes globalised trade and intensive agriculture which is an indirect driver of poverty and biodiversity loss. There is power and consequences in all of our choices and decisions. For me, it is time to start respecting each other and the animals with the greatest care. Animals are not commodities; they are sentient beings. In short, a really strong, unified, informed commitment to regeneration and protection of the environment for this one Earth is crucial (for all the human and other than human beings, as Satish would say). Biodiverse multi-functional sea, water and landscapes are more resilient. We can transform our hearts and renew our minds towards a place of peace with the Earth and with each other.

A candle of hope is being lit as the local community café also houses a repair café to counteract the throw-away culture. Planting trees and hedgerows is organised by the council. More pollinator strips are noticeable as well as a small-scale organic farm. Another idea is to plant fruit trees to re-establish the traditional orchards that were once part of this area's identity. If you walk the quiet back roads you can see remnants of the old fruit trees that were grubbed up in the 1970s in the UK due to increasing commercialisation and subsidies (Hansard, 1976). The local school is making sure that a garden to learn how to grow vegetables, and flowers to attract pollinators are available and running within the school grounds. A day of closing the road to vehicles so that all the children could cycle their bikes safely to school took a lot of initiative and planning from one teacher but brought so much joy to the community. This reminds me of Satish's concern for children's education which we discussed on the pilgrimage. He was forward thinking in starting the Small School in Hartland, Devon (1982-2017) for 11-16-year-olds. It was a co-educational independent school to ensure that young people could (alongside the curriculum) also be aware of how to grow organic food and plants from seed and how to cook vegetarian food (cooking, sharing food and cleaning up with parents). They had options such as learning yoga, pottery, woodwork and dance. Learning in nature included climbing trees in the garden, swimming in the river and days visiting on foot areas of natural beauty. There is strong evidence that exposure to nature is linked to good health and overall wellbeing (Sandifer, Sutton-Grier and Ward, 2015) because we *are* nature. The Small School had the benefit of small class sizes so every young person could be heard, respected and have freedom of expression, imagination and creativity. This personalised approach can be contrasted to secondary schools that focus so strongly on academic attainment rather than nature and nurture, fun, life skills and useable craft. This type of guidance must help promote confidence and independent thought, a different outlook on life. To be hot-housed only for attainment is not looking at the young person's wellbeing, happiness or how they treat others when they participate in life on this planet. The school is now going to be a centre for education, environment and the arts. It will also house the *Resurgence* office. This will be the base for the vital, relevant and poetic

Resurgence & Ecologist magazine. *Resurgence* celebrates conservation, culture, ecology and spirituality. It is most exciting that sustainable organic food production, creative outdoor classrooms for children and nature conservation are being planned for this centre.

Satish Kumar offers a path for others to follow towards a more compassionate, regenerative and equal society. For me, this path has allowed me to connect Satish Kumar with Jagdish Rattanani and Dr. Sudarshan Iyengar, and to reconnect him with his partner in walking for world peace, E.P. Menon, who lives in Bengaluru in Southern India. Thank you from my heart for taking time out to weave this story together.

References

Sandifer, P.A., Sutton-Grier, A.E. & Ward, B.P. (2015) 'Exploring connections among nature, biodiversity and human health and wellbeing: Opportunities and biodiversity conservation.' *Ecosystem Services*, 12, pp.1-15.

Schumacher, E.F. (1993) *Small is Beautiful: A study of economics as if people mattered.* Vintage Books.

Hansard (1976) 'Horticulture (Apple And Pear Growers) (Special Payments) (Variation) Scheme'. Available at: https://bit.ly/Satish12

United Nations (2016) 'Harmony with Nature' [online]. Available at: https://bit.ly/Satish07

World People's Conference on Climate Change and the Mother Earth (2010) Rights of Mother Earth [online]. Available at: https://pwccc.wordpress.com/programa

THE CONVERSATIONS

CHAPTER 1:

Around the Globe, Footloose, Penniless

The year is 1962. Two young Indian men, inspired by nothing more than a newspaper clipping, decide to set off on foot across the globe. They would walk for the next two and a half years, their pugnacious dreams including audiences with world leaders such as Nikita Khrushchev in the USSR and Charles de Gaulle in France, to pass on to them the message of peace. It is the time of the Cold War, with the world fairly riven in half, either on the side of the USA or the Soviet Union, both sides stockpiling nuclear weapons.

One of the men is Satish Kumar, for whom leaving the beaten track was nothing very new. At nine he had become a monk, at eighteen he left monkhood to become a Gandhian. The globe walk was just one of the many turning points in his life.

Interviewers: How did the idea of footing it around the globe come about?

Satish: I was in Bangalore at that time, and my friend and colleague E.P. Menon and I were at a coffee house. We had ordered coffee and began to discuss a news item in the papers that day. The ninety-year-old British philosopher and Nobel Prize winner, Lord Bertrand Russell, had been put in jail because he was demonstrating against nuclear weapons and working for peace. It gave me goose-pimples. Imagine, a man of ninety going to jail for peace in the world.

What are we doing, young men sitting here drinking coffee? We must do something. And we talked and talked and talked. In the end, after talking for about an hour (we forgot the coffee!), we decided we must join the international peace movement led by people like Bertrand Russell. This was the height of the Cold War and the tension between the United States of America and the Soviet Union was very strong; at any time, a nuclear accident or nuclear war could have happened. So, at that time, saving the world from a nuclear catastrophe was the biggest challenge globally.

We asked ourselves what we could do. We decided to walk to four nuclear capitals of the world. We had never been abroad, neither my friend nor I. We were in India sitting in this coffee house and dreaming about walking to Moscow, to Paris, to London and to Washington DC, and we felt excited. Let's do it. Whatever happens, let's do it. It is a long story; you have to read my book.

We went to Vinoba (Bhave) for his approval and blessings. And Vinoba said, "Yes. Wonderful idea, go. But – big condition – go without any money in your pocket."

Wars have their beginnings in fear. Why are there conflicts, why are there nuclear weapons? Because Russia is afraid of America, and America is afraid of Russia. Fear creates bombs, weapons, conflicts, wars. So, if you want an antidote to fear, that is trust, Vinoba said. And you don't want to just go and talk about peace, you have to *be* peace, be an example of peace. When you have no money, that means you have to trust yourself, trust the world, trust nature, trust the universe, the process of the universe. So, go with trust. Fill your rucksack, not with money but with trust. Fill your heart with trust and go.

Now, Vinoba was our guru. And you are not a dilettante with your guru, that you take advice only when it suits you, when you like it. We said it is a very difficult advice but we will do it. So we took all the money out of our pockets, and started walking from the grave of Mahatma Gandhi. We had tremendous support from the Indian government, the media, the Gandhian movement ... much support. We walked through north India, through Punjab and arrived at the border of India and Pakistan. This was the last day for us in India. Lots of people were worried about how we were going to survive, and they came to say goodbye and to fare us well.

There was one dear friend, Kranti, who said, "Satish, I am very worried. Are you crazy? You are going to Pakistan, our enemy country. We have had three wars between India and Pakistan over Kashmir. Muslims don't like Hindus, they don't like non-Muslims. How are you going to survive? At least you should take some food with you." She had brought some packets of food. "And I will give you some money."

That was a challenging moment. She was a very dear friend of mine, most dear. I thought for a minute, then I remembered Vinoba. He had said, "Have no fear, just trust."

And I said to Kranti, "I'm afraid I cannot take these parcels of food. These are not parcels of food, they are parcels of mistrust. What am I going to say to my Pakistani host – that I did not trust you, as to whether you will feed me or not, so I have come with my own food all the way from India? This is not trust, this is fear." Kranti started to cry. She said, "Satish, you are going without money, without food, walking, through Muslim, Christian, communist, capitalist countries, deserts, mountains, forests. How are you going to survive? This might be our last meeting, I might never see you again."

That was a very, very emotional moment for me, but I said to my friend, "Look, we have taken a decision; we have to take a risk. To live is to risk. You cannot live a life without it. And going for peace is a risk; better I die than the whole world dies with nuclear weapons. So, if I don't get food, I will say this is my opportunity to fast. If I don't get shelter, I will say this is my opportunity to sleep under the stars. And that will be my million-star hotel instead of the five-star hotel.

And if I die, which you are afraid of, Kranti, I will say this is the best kind of death I can have, dying while walking for peace. So, I will adhere to Vinoba's teachings of trust. And let me go." She gave me a hug, in tears.

I: What were your most memorable experiences from that walk?

Satish: There are lots of stories from our walk, but in Pakistan we had a wonderful reception, and people walked with us, Muslims. Their soldiers and armies had fought against the Indian army. But we were peacemakers. They said, we want peace between India and Pakistan. So, for a whole month we were walking, sometimes at night, without fear, under the moonlight, and people would come with us.

They would take us to the next stage and find us contacts. We are so afraid of Pakistan ... I said to my friends, "If we come here as Indians, we meet Pakistanis; if we come here as Hindus, we meet Muslims; but if we come here as human beings, we meet human beings. So, what is our identity? Not Indian, Gandhian, Jain, Buddhist, Hindu, this and that. Our primary identity is that we are human beings. And then our secondary identities are fine, no problem. But if we just adhere to secondary identities then we have divisions and quarrels and conflicts and fights and wars."

We walked through Pakistan and Afghanistan, through the Afghan mountains. Afghanistan was a peaceful country at that time, a beautiful country. There was no war. And it had a king.

And then we walked through Iran, through the deserts. We could not see two metres away; it was dusty and so full of sandstorms in the salt desert. We travelled through that to Teheran. We were there for a hundred days, walking through Iran. We had a lot of difficulties; sometimes there was no water, sometimes no food, sometimes visa problems ... many problems. Finally, we came to Azerbaijan and Armenia.

The Georgian woman and her peace tea

Satish: One story that was amazing was that of peace tea. We used to give leaflets to our hosts or to anybody we saw in the streets. We did not speak all the languages, so we translated, and our embassies helped us to translate our leaflets. We had translations in Persian, Russian and many languages. When we were in Georgia, we gave a Russian leaflet to two women who were standing in front of a tea factory. They read it, and as we were walking away they called out and said, "Stop, stop, tell us a bit more. You have walked all the way from India, all the way, walking?"

We started to talk a little in our broken Russian, and they said, "You have no money. Where do you eat? Do you want some food, or some tea? We work in this tea factory, we have a canteen. Would you like some lunch? We have a lunch break." Any time is tea time for us, we told them. We would have some tea. So we went in. They sat around us and wanted to know our story. They brought us tea, bread, jam ... lovely, very nice. Then suddenly, after about twenty minutes, when we had finished our tea and were about to leave, they asked whether we could wait a minute. One of the women went out of the room and came back with four packets of tea, and said, "These packets of tea are not for you."

She said: "I would like you to be my messenger and I would like you to deliver one packet of tea to our premier in the Kremlin. The second packet of tea to the president of France in Palace Elysée. The third packet of tea to the prime minister of England at 10 Downing Street, and the fourth packet to the president of the USA in Washington DC at the White House. And please give them a message from me. I am an ordinary woman working here in a tea factory, I will never reach there, I cannot even dream of reaching there, but you are going. You said you are going to Moscow, Paris, London and Washington. So please go to these four places, headquarters of the governments of the nuclear powers, and give them a message from me."

This was an ordinary woman in a small tea factory by the Black Sea in Georgia. She said, "I have a message for Khrushchev, for John Kennedy, de Gaulle, and the prime minister of England. My message to them is that if ever you get the mad thought of pressing the nuclear button, please stop for a moment and have a fresh cup of tea (there was much laughter at this). And that will give you a moment to reflect and realise that your nuclear weapons are not legal, because war can only be fought between two armies, and nuclear weapons will kill men, women, children, ordinary citizens, not only humans, but also animals, forests, lakes, rivers ... everything will be contaminated." An ordinary woman working in a tea factory, giving such a profound message to deliver to the Kremlin and the White House!

You cannot imagine my inspiration and my amazement at this woman's gesture. So I said, "Now, whatever the problem – hunger, snow, rain, storm, sleeplessness, homelessness – whatever the problem, now we have a mission. Now our mission is to deliver these four packets of tea to these four nuclear capitals of the world." That was an amazing encounter.

I: So, were you able to deliver those packets?

Satish: When we arrived in Moscow, we wrote to Khrushchev, and Khrushchev wrote us back, saying, "I cannot see you because I am not free, but I am appointing the President of the Supreme Soviet and he will receive you in the Kremlin. Please come." And so we went.

We delivered the first packet of peace tea at the Kremlin to the president of the Supreme Soviet. He said, "Of course we are for peace. Russia lost something like 15 million citizens in World War II, a huge number of deaths. So, we will never dream of war. But we have to protect ourselves against America. Go to America."

"We are going to America", I said, "But we want you to show an example. Unilateral disarmament." They would not listen.

In jail in France

Satish: Anyway, we continued our walk. We walked through Russia, Poland, Germany, Belgium and France. In France we met a hurdle. President de Gaulle said we will have nothing to do with you and nothing to do with peace tea.

The USA, Britain and Russia had signed the test ban treaty. They agreed not to conduct nuclear tests anymore. But France had refused. If they were not prepared to listen to these three governments, then who were we that they should heed us. De Gaulle would not meet us. So we went to demonstrate in front of Elysée Palace with our banners, accompanied by some twenty or thirty French people, pacifists. We were arrested there and put in jail in Paris. We said to ourselves, never mind, we are following in the footsteps of Bertrand Russell, and Mahatma Gandhi before, who was for a very long time in prison. Bertrand Russell was our inspiration. We spent three nights in jail. The head of police told us, "Look, either we have to send you back to India or, what do we do with you, you carry on … Give me your peace tea and I will see if I can deliver it to Palace Elysée somehow. You carry on."

I: What was the response of the Indian government to all this?

Satish: Very good. Jawaharlal Nehru (the then Prime Minister) himself wrote a letter and ordered the Foreign Department to give us passports without any security. Nehru himself asked his Foreign Office to write to all our embassies to receive us and to help us in case of any problem. In Tehran we were received by our ambassador, and by our ambassador T.N. Kaul in Moscow. There was G.M. Dhameja in Kabul. Nehru was supportive, Sarvepalli Radhakrishnan (the then President) was supportive. The newspapers wrote about us.

Among the foreign governments, the Shah of Iran met us personally. But the only person who totally rejected us was De Gaulle. Otherwise, the others, even if they did not meet us themselves, at least they deputed someone important.

We carried on. From Calais to Dover we took a boat … the French people helped us, and from Dover we walked to London. We were received in the House of Commons by the representative of the prime minister of England, Lord Attlee, and we delivered the packet of peace tea to him.

Face to face with Bertrand Russell

Satish: Then we met Bertrand Russell. He had written to us before, in response to our letter, when we started our journey, saying that we were inspired by him. He said, "When I wrote to you, when I received your letter, I never thought that I will be alive to see you. I was ninety years old at that time, now I am ninety-two. But you have walked fast." He was very, very gracious.

We spent the night in his village. He said, "You walked all the way without money from India, because it was overland, you could walk. You can't go to America without money. Can I help you?" We told him we had not touched money for two years, so we could not take any money. But if he could help us get two tickets on a boat, as we did not want to fly, we would be very grateful.

Lord Russell turned to his PA and asked him to help us. We were given two tickets on the *Queen Mary* and we sailed across the Atlantic. We arrived in New York, and then we walked from New York to Washington, DC. We were received at the White House by the representative of the president of the USA, and we delivered our packet of peace tea at the White House.

We finished our journey at the grave of John F. Kennedy at Arlington. From the grave of Mahatma Gandhi to the grave of John F. Kennedy, two graves, grave to grave, to make the point that if you believe in the gun, which is the beginning of the nuclear bomb, a gun kills not only a bad person but can also kill a Gandhi or a Kennedy. We made the point that you must remove your faith in the gun and have faith in peace and negotiation and solution through conversation. Here we ended our journey.

An audience with the legendary Martin Luther King

Satish: We were received by Martin Luther King. There was a wonderful aura of peace about him. He said, "India is my inspiration." Mahatma Gandhi's picture was hanging on the wall behind his desk.

Then he said, "What I learned from Mahatma Gandhi is that non-violence is not only a technique to protest against injustice, but non-violence is a way of life." And that was a wonderful message to hear from Martin Luther King. That's what I believe, that's what Mahatma Gandhi believed; also, that peace is not only absence of war, peace is a way of life. Non-violence and peace – those were the principles of Mahatma Gandhi which I carried on my journey.

Onwards to Hiroshima

Satish: Then we received an invitation from Japan. A Buddhist group there told us we could not go back to India without making a pilgrimage to Hiroshima. Hiroshima was the first victim of the nuclear weapon, and then Nagasaki. We came to Tokyo, and there many Buddhist monks joined us and there was a tremendous reception all over Japan for forty-five days. We walked from Tokyo to Hiroshima, and every day hundreds of people lined the street welcoming us, hundreds of people listening to our message. We had wonderful hospitality and we went to Hiroshima as our concluding destination. Then, with the help of the Buddhists in Japan, who gave us two tickets on a boat, we returned to Bombay, India. My friend Kranti came to see me, to welcome me at the port in Bombay. She was so happy that we had returned alive in spite of all the problems and difficulties along our way.

I: That was a really bold journey on your part. But was it not very frustrating that none of the heads of these four great states would meet with you to receive the peace tea? Of course, unfortunately, Kennedy died.

Satish: Yes, it was sad. We would have welcomed being received by Khrushchev and Johnson and all. But one had to accept the situation as it was. And these people are so busy, they are powerful and they want to meet others equal to them – heads of state or some special persons. But we were vagabonds, peaceniks carrying bags of peace tea – for them it was a very small matter. At least Khrushchev wrote a letter, signed by himself, and said that the president of the Supreme Soviet will meet you in the Kremlin and I have urged my fellow and my colleague who is the Supreme Soviet Chairman to meet you. And then Khrushchev's personal assistant phoned us. So that was a kind of middle way – not extreme success, but something. But at that time, who were we? At least now you can say that Satish Kumar has written some books, got some awards, started Schumacher College, I have something under my belt as a sign of my labour. But at that time, I was nothing. I was a twenty-six-year-old, and *deewana* or *pagal* – mad, a vagabond.

I: I am especially curious about your walking through the Middle East. I am wondering whether a woman could do it in today's world.

Satish: I would say, like we two men did it, two women would be better. In India we have a saying: *Dhyanam ekaki, Gamanam dwity, Gayanam tridhi,* which means: meditation alone, travelling or walking two, singing three. If you are walking or travelling, it is always good to have a companion. I don't think being a woman is any impediment. Man or woman, it doesn't matter. You need courage, conviction, resilience. You can do it. I don't think God made women to be weak or fearful. No, we are equal. There is no difference. Men and women are complementary; we need two to create the third.

And there are many examples. A woman, Dervla Murphy, bicycled alone from Dublin to Delhi through the Middle East. She went through Turkey, Iran, Afghanistan and Pakistan to Delhi. So, from Dublin to Delhi, one woman, bicycling. And then she went to Africa. There was a peace pilgrim in America, a woman, who walked across all of America for twenty years. My pilgrimage is nothing, for two and a half years. Twenty years, one woman, a single woman, walked, just with a toothbrush and one change of clothes, nothing else, no money. There is a book about it, *Peace Pilgrim*, you can read it. I would not say being a woman in any way is an impediment or an obstacle for any adventure.

Mother Teresa, what did she do? What a wonderful journey of life, how many obstacles and difficulties she faced. But one woman ... she did a wonderful job. Wangari Maathai was one woman, planting 20 million trees. So, women can achieve more than men can. All women are heroes. All mothers are heroes. Giving birth to a child, what a great risk they take, in the life-and-death experience of giving birth to a child. Your question is good, but please do not think that being a woman is any impediment to making a peace pilgrimage. You can go through the Middle East ... you will have some difficulties, visas, and some problems. But if you have the will, there will be a way. Determination was our greatest strength, and with that determination, whatever problem came, we faced it.

We said, any problem is an opportunity to be patient, to be forgiving and to be resilient. If everything was smooth, and everything was arranged and all the hotels were booked, and everywhere there were reception committees welcoming us, there is no adventure. Adventure is to take risks and go through difficulties.

Difficulties are part of any pilgrimage. Our journey was not all smooth. I have told you some nice stories, but we faced bullets twice in our journey, gunpoint twice. There were many days when we were thrown out of homes, at night, midnight, and told you can't stay here. We faced many problems, visas got refused. Whether you are a man or a woman, problems will be there and the problems will make you strong and resilient. Don't be afraid of problems. If you want to do something, just do it.

I: What is the difference between the times when you did your peace walk against the nuclear threat and now, during the times of Brexit and this fear of 'the other'? Today, in England and in the world, hate and fear have other shapes, like the fear of refugees or fear of sharing territory or having one's culture overrun.

Satish: Fear of an enemy like Russia or the USA, or fear of communism or capitalism, fear of migrants, refugees, fear of being overwhelmed by others. The fear is the same, only the format is changed. From a Gandhian perspective, sharing is the solution. Poverty in the world is not because there is lack of money or food. There is no lack of food, money, space, air, water. What is lacking is sharing. Even in the United States, with so much wealth, the number one economy in the world, they still don't share. There is poverty.

They fear migrants. They say we want to get this wall built between Mexico and the United States. That is fear. What is lacking? There is so much land in the United States that if you put the entire world population of seven billion people in there, it will not be denser than the population density of India. Such a huge country ... they have everything and yet they are not prepared to share. Never mind foreigners, the Americans themselves are poor, they have no education, no medicine or medical insurance, no security of life. There is a lot of poverty and homelessness, misery and deprivation, in America. If they are such a rich country and they have not been able to solve the problems of poverty, hunger, misery and deprivation, what hope is there for any other country?

The solution to fear is sharing. You share with all human beings. What is America? It is made up of people from 50 to 70 nations and they have all come as migrants. If you don't want migrants, then you go away yourself! Trump, go back to Scotland. Why are you in America? You are a foreigner. But that is not the point. Most people in the US are foreigners, migrants, they have come one day or the other, and the American Indians welcomed them in the beginning. There were wars and fights, but originally the American Indians were welcoming. If they could be so generous, why are you being so mean now? In India, we are all seeking economic growth, 5% to 10% economic growth. But even if India became as rich as America, and the number one economy, our poverty will not go away, because we are not sharing.

In Mumbai, there is no shortage of wealth and yet we have slums and shanties, because we are not sharing. So the Gandhian solution is to rise above one's fear of migrants, refugees, of the other, of the poor, and to share. When you share, fear will go away. Everybody is a human being, everybody needs a small amount of food, they only need one or two pairs of clothes, and if we share there will be enough for everybody. The Gandhian solution is to share, whereas the capitalist system is to hoard. Accumulate and hoard, for myself.

There is a goddess in India called Annapurna*. *Anna* is food, *purna* is plenty, so she is the goddess of plentifulness of food. She is sitting in the kitchens of those who are prepared to share. The moment you start to share, food will keep emerging; there will be no end to the food. That is the Indian idea. That is a Gandhian idea. If you share, food will never be in shortage. But if you start hoarding, everything will be in shortage. So sharing is the solution.

Chapter 2:

Monk at Nine

Walking everywhere for two and a half years was hardly new to Satish Kumar. He had done this for nine years as a boy-monk with his master.

Although not unknown in the Jain tradition, Satish Kumar decided to become a monk at the incredibly tender age of nine. Life had dealt him an early blow, leaving him wracked with existential questions. Spirituality seemed the only path.

I: Your decision to become a monk at nine ... that was a really early decision, considering it was completely voluntary.

Satish: The first of my memories is when I was four. Of seeing my father dead and my mother crying. The first memory of my life is a very sad one. And I am asking my mother, "Why is father not talking to me, why he is not walking, why just lying down there, and why are you crying? And you have removed all the jewellery you used to wear. And you are wearing this dark sari, while you used to wear beautiful saris. What has happened?"

And my mother said, "I am sorry, sad to tell you that your father is dead."

"What does that mean? What is dead?"

"He is never going to talk to you anymore. He will never be with us anymore. And this is why I am crying."

He was only about 50 years. He had a heart attack. That experience of seeing the death of my father and the tears of my mother made me very sad. From that time, my mother used to tell me, I was a very sad-looking boy and did not take much interest in playing or anything else.

My mother was a very devout Jain and she used to pay visits to Jain monks. On one of her trips – I was by now six or seven years old – she took me to see our Jain guru. While my mother was busy with something else, I approached this guru. He was sitting alone. I took some courage and I said to him, "Can I ask you something?"

He was a bit surprised at a young boy of seven asking to speak to him. "What do you want to ask?"

I said, "My father is dead, my mother is very sad, I am very sad. Is there any way of stopping people dying?"

To cut the long story of our conversation short, he said, "Yes, there is a way of stopping people dying. Maybe not in this life but in the long term."

"And what is the way?"

"The way is to renounce the world, all attachments, all possessions, and live a very pure, non-violent, simple, monk's life. Then you do not accumulate any karma, and karma is a kind of cycle, of action and reaction. When you become a monk – and this is why we have become monks so that we don't come back into the world – there is no birth, no death, very simple."

At that time, it seemed very simple to me, so I said, "Can I become a monk?"

I went to my mother and I said, "Mother, I want to stop people dying. I want to stop this cycle of birth and death and ever and ever, never ending, people dying, people crying. I want to stop it."

My mother, seeing that I was a seven- or eight-year-old boy, did not take much notice. But she was a devout Jain and understood what I was talking about. I said to her that our guru says that you can stop the cycle of birth and death by renouncing the world and by becoming a monk.

Fortunately, within a year, our guru came to our town for *chaturmas** – the four months of the monsoon period. And my mother, sisters and many people from the town went to receive him outside the town. And I saw this guru with his followers emerging from behind the sand dunes ... handsome; he was only about thirty years old, with an amazing presence. I had no father, so I felt he is my father, such an amazing man. Everybody was praising him, singing songs. Not only did I want to be free of birth and death, I wanted to be with him, such a wonderful guru, like my father. So, eventually, to tell you briefly, I said to my mother that this monsoon period, when our guru is here, at this time and during this period, I will become a monk.

My brother was very much against it. My sister said, "What are you talking about? You are only nine years old."

But my mother said, "I will be sad to lose you but your path is very good. You are following a very great religious, spiritual path." Being a devout Jain, she understood. She was torn. In one way she was losing her son, on the other hand her son was taking this amazing, wonderful spiritual path, spiritual journey, so she was also proud.

In the end, I became a monk at age nine.

I: Do you remember anything of those first months? At nine, you might have been sad at being separated from your loved ones. But it was your own decision too.

Satish: I remember the day I became a monk, absolutely vividly, like a picture in front of my eyes. It was my own decision. I wanted to become a monk because I liked my guru and I was very inspired.

And I remember my mother had four kilos of gold and she said the four kilos were for her four children. When you become a monk, you leave the world. So I want to give you this one kilo of gold, she told me. As a monk, I could not carry any gold, and she wanted to get rid of that gold as she had decided that that one kilo of gold was for me. So, I said and she agreed, that the gold would be turned into rings. There must have been more than a hundred of them – and I would give a ring as a memento of my becoming a monk to friends, family, sisters, brothers, uncles, aunts, nieces, nephews, neighbours, teachers, fellow students, to whoever I met, till they were finished. Giving away the rings was also a symbol of renunciation for me.

I: Very unusual for a boy of nine to do all this.

Satish: Yes. Sometimes the inspiration comes. You never know. My mother was a great blessing to me. She was a wonderful mother. She always encouraged me to think, to imagine.

To come back to the question of my years as a monk ... being a monk for nine years gave me a very good foundation. It was a very good training for me, in that you can live without a home, without money, without shoes, without many clothes (because I had only one change of clothes and one begging bowl), and just walk every day. I wasn't allowed to use a bullock cart or ride a bicycle or take a boat or train or car, nothing. For nine years I walked barefoot on the ground, begging for food – and no monastery – with my guru, Acharya Tulsi.

I: So, you were a monk from age nine to the age of 18?

Satish: Right. I became a Jain monk with Acharya Tulsi at age nine and I was there until age 18. And those nine years gave me strength and resilience. I could live for nine years without a penny in my pocket. I could live for nine years just by begging for food and eating once a day.

I: This would be completely away from your home and parents?

Satish: Away from home. Home is no longer my home. Parents are no longer my parents. And for nine years I was a monk, barefoot and walking. We could only go over the bridge if there was a bridge; otherwise you stayed on this side of the river. And complete non-violence. I wore a little mask over my mouth so that I wouldn't hurt any insects outside, held a little brush in my hand, to brush away ants or insects in my path before I put my foot down. I would not sit on the grass. I would not have shoes. And always a begging bowl. I had one change of clothes which I carried on my back and carried one begging bowl.

I would go from door to door begging for food. And if somebody gave me two chapatis, I'd say only one. So never take too much from one house, a little here and a little there. It is said that a monk begs for food as a honey bee takes nectar from the flower. The flower is never harmed. The honey bee goes from flower to flower, taking a little nectar here and a little there, never too much. Never has a flower to complain that the honey bee took too much nectar away.

So I had a begging bowl, was barefoot, and my robe was white and unstitched.

I: And what geographical areas did you cover? Do you remember those?

Satish: I covered most of Rajasthan, I went to Jodhpur, Udaipur, Bikaner, Ajmer, Agra, Delhi, Ambala, Ludhiana, Patiala, Jhansi, Hisar. So maybe I would say Haryana, Punjab, Rajasthan, parts of Uttar Pradesh, and Delhi. That is the area I covered in nine years. Every day I covered seven to ten miles.

I: What had you to do the whole day?

Satish: My teacher Acharya Tulsi would teach; I was his student. My main training was to learn to meditate. I learned ten thousand verses of Sanskrit, and of Prakrit, which is the text language of the Jains. I learned the Dashwaikalik Sutra*, the Uttaradhyen Sutra*, the Acharan Sutra*, all by heart. And then I learned many other religious texts in Sanskrit and Prakrit. Then Acharya would also teach me how to teach. On our walks over sand dunes or through a forest, sometimes we would sit on a dune or under a tree, and he would say, now, you have heard me speak many times, speak about non-violence, and think that there are about two hundred people in front of you, and they don't know anything about non-violence, particularly the Jain idea of non-violence, or anything –

*aparigraha** or *anekanta**. He would give me a title for the talk and would say, speak now, and I would speak. There would be nobody there except for him and a few monks, and I would speak for ten or fifteen minutes, just for practice. He would do that quite often, to teach me how to preach, how to teach, how to speak. That had been good training for me, and I can speak without any notes and improvise.

I: But in the early days it would be received wisdom. You would receive something and in some way regurgitate it. Isn't it?

Satish: Acharya Tulsi did not encourage me to repeat him, he encouraged me to think, and to speak from my heart. No notes. "Speak from your heart," he would say, "about how you understand any subject, how you understand peace, non-violence, *aparigraha*..." He would provide me a random subject and ask me to speak what I thought. Don't think about what your guru has said, he would say. He was encouraging, he was a very good teacher. I was very fortunate to have him as my teacher. The text would be written, and I would learn during the day. What I had learned during the day I would recall without reading the last thing before going to bed. Then first thing when I woke up at 4 a.m. or 4.30 a.m., I would try to remember what I had learned the previous day. Then I would have forty-five minutes to one hour of meditation, mostly chanting Jain mantras. When you are chanting, your focus is on that chant and the words and the meaning of the words. Then chanting brings you enchantment. So you transcend any kind of thinking, worrying about problems. So that was mantra, meditation, chanting, remembering what you learned from the old religious texts. On most days Acharya Tulsi would go somewhere to preach, so I would go along to hear him. And that was a learning process … a very good foundation.

I: If you had not left the monkhood, would those have been your activities even today?

Satish: That is kind of speculation, it is hypothetical. If I had not left, I think I would still encourage people to take care of the Earth, make peace with nature and the environment. I imagine that would still be my interest. And I would continue. But perhaps I would also be sad at being disconnected from the world, aloof from the world.

CHAPTER 3:

Back in the World

As the prized disciple of his guru, Satish Kumar appeared to be entrenched in the Jain order. A chance encounter with a Gandhian follower and a chance reading of Gandhi shook his ideas of life. The material world is not a trap and one can live a spiritual life without withdrawing from the world, he realised. But to engage in worldly affairs again meant breaking the vow of renunciation, which would hurt those who mattered the most to him.

I: When did you begin to feel that you could be with the world and still follow a spiritual path? Was this behind your decision to leave your life as a monk?

Satish: My life was transformed by Mahatma Gandhi's autobiography, *My Experiments with Truth* [*Satya Ke Sath Mere Prayog*]. Someone gave me that book. What I learnt from it was that in order to practise spirituality you don't have to renounce the world. How many people can renounce the world? How many people can go and live in a monastic order? Only a few. The majority of people have to live in the world in their day-to-day lives. Spirituality should be such that by changing your motivation, changing your intention, changing your purpose, you transform everything in your life into spiritual practice. So, your politics becomes spiritual, if you are not doing it out of ego, or for prestige, power, name, fame or control, but as a pure service. If you are not doing business for money, profit, gain, fame, ego, but for pure service to the community, you could be a spiritual businessman. A teacher, who is not teaching as a job, but teaching to empower students – that is a spiritual teacher. If you are a doctor not taking medicine as a job or profession but as a vocation, healing people, bringing good health to people ... If it is in the service of humanity that you are a doctor, a teacher, a businessman or farmer, whatever your profession ... (you are following the spiritual path).

Mahatma Gandhi created this understanding for me. He said you don't have to go and live in a cave or live in a monastery to be spiritual. You can be in a cave and be still attached and be self-centred.

The world is not a trap

Everything that we do in life can be spiritual if we do it with the right intention and right motivation. You are doing it in the service of humanity, with no ego but with humility, only giving and receiving – there is reciprocity, but you do not desire for your own self gain. So I was very impressed, inspired. I said, this is amazing. I am looking at the world as if it is a trap, a dirty world, and (believe) I have to free myself from the world to bring an end to birth and death. But not everybody can do this, and there are billions of people in the world. So I was very inspired by Mahatma Gandhi.

By being in the service of others, you liberate yourself, enlighten yourself and purify yourself. By not concentrating on the self but on the service of others, you are actually benefiting yourself. That is the paradox. And that was Gandhi. I was inspired by Gandhi, so I left the monastic order.

But when you become a monk you take the vow for life. I had to break the vow, and I knew that would hurt my mother and would hurt my guru. They would see it as a kind of betrayal, which it was in a way. But I was so passionate and inspired by the teachings of Mahatma Gandhi that one night, after midnight, when the whole town was asleep, everybody was asleep, I escaped.

As a monk, I had also met Vinoba Bhave. As part of his *bhoodan yatra* [journey], he had camped in Delhi at Raj Ghat, a memorial in Delhi dedicated to Mahatma Gandhi. That was in 1953 or 1954. I was in Delhi with my guru, Acharya Tulsi. And there was a very wonderful Hindi writer, a Jain, called Jainendra Kumar, and he was the bridge. He knew Vinoba and he was a follower of my guru. He said to Vinoba, "I would like you to meet our Jain *acharya* [*a leader, in this case of the Jain order, used generally as an honorific before the name of teachers*]." Vinoba and Acharya Tulsi knew of each other but hadn't met. When Acharya Tulsi went to meet Vinoba, he took me with him. In their conversation Vinoba asked my guru something and Acharya said, "And we teach Sanskrit". And he asked me to speak for four or five minutes in Sanskrit, about the importance of work as a gift – *dana*. Vinoba was pleased and he looked at me, and I was very impressed with Vinoba.

And so, having met Vinoba, and having read Gandhi, I became very unsettled, very anxious and very inspired, all together. I left the monastic order. I went to Bodhgaya* and stayed in the Samanvaya ashram. Dwarko Sundrani [*who before his passing on March 31, 2021, was regarded as the last active disciple of Mahatma Gandhi*] was a fellow member of my community, an elder and a very good guide.

In Vinoba's fold, with a new name

Vinoba, my new guru, had this ashram in Bihar, in Bodhgaya, a Buddhist place. He gave me refuge. He was walking, and I joined him, so it was like being a monk. Living in the ashram, I learned to cook and to garden and I walked with Vinoba from village to village. Rather than begging for food, now I was begging for land. Not for myself but for the landless people. So Vinoba and many of us would go to a landlord and say, "If you have five children, consider Vinoba as your sixth child, and give one-sixth of your land for the poor."

And it was a miracle. If you want to know a miracle, read the story of Vinoba. There is also a book, *Moved by Love,* on the life of Vinoba. Thousands joined him. Vinoba walked more than 100,000 kilometres, north, south, east, west, centre, all over India – 100,000 kilometres for 13 years. The miracle was, he was given four million acres of land, which was distributed to the landless poor. That was a wonderful experience for me. This is how my Gandhian ideas were formulated, and I learnt from Vinoba, for I had never met Gandhi. Vinoba became my teacher, and he was a great friend and also mentor of Gandhi. Sometimes, if Gandhi was worrying or was in a dilemma or confused and needed some advice, he would go to Vinoba and say, "What should I do in this situation?" And Vinoba would advise him. He was much younger than Gandhi. He was a very pure human being.

I: I am very curious to know – Acharya Tulsi being what he was, an outstanding Jain personality, would he, considering your position, have allowed you to go? Was it your youth in those days that made you leave?

Satish: No, no, Acharya Tulsi was totally against my leaving the monastic order.

I: Did you speak to him about it?

Satish: No, I did not. And when I left the monastic order, not only was Acharya Tulsi very upset, you may say he was almost angry with me. But he was very upset with Vinoba, and he sent a message or messenger to Vinoba to say, don't allow our monks to go and find refuge in your ashrams because that way it will encourage our monks to leave the order and become your members, and that will not be good for us and it will not be good for Jains. But Vinoba did not accept that argument and he said nothing doing, his ashram is for all religions.

And then he said to me, "Satish, your past is now gone. You must change your name." My original name was Bhairudaan and Vinoba changed my name to Satish. And he told me not to call myself by any caste* name or any religious name, like Jain or something. You are you, nothing else. And he said to Tulsi, "If your monks want to come and live in our ashram, they are welcome." So there was a tug-of-war, a little bit of tension there. Even though Tulsi was outstanding, a very wonderful teacher as far as his order was concerned, he was a bit dogmatic, in the sense that he did not want his monks to leave and disobey.

I: You would not have faced him after deciding to leave?

Satish: He sent a lot of his followers to me and tried to persuade me to meet him but I knew he would be angry so I did not go to him. But when I went around the world for peace without money, and walking, that impressed him. That was many years later, because I left the monkhood in 1954, and I did the walk 1962 to 1964, so there was a gap of 10 years. He was very good and he praised me to my mother. He said, "What your son has done is very wonderful. I was very upset, but what he has done is wonderful. I admire it." My mother was very pleased. She came to see me. I was in Varanasi at that time, having returned after my journey, and was working at the Gandhi Seva Sangh. I was working with Siddaraj Dhadda [*a noted peace leader who was later honoured for his social and constructive work*]. My mother travelled all the way from Bikaner, Rajasthan State, by herself, changing trains at New Delhi and Mughalsarai, and came to Varanasi, without announcement, without any letter. She knocked at my door and said, "I have come to forgive you. And Acharya Tulsi was happy with you." But I still did not dare to go and see him, concerned that he would not be happy.

I: Was your mother was very upset?

Satish: Yes, my mother was very upset.

I: How was your meeting with your mother that day, when she arrived?

Satish: Amazing. I loved my mother very much. My mother was a wonderful, wise person. When she came, I was so touched, and in tears. And I said, "Mother, I can have new friends, I can have a new job, I can have anything new, but I cannot have a new mother. And you not accepting me was a great loss for me. So you coming here is very great." So that was wonderful. And there was great forgiveness from her, and the happiness was mutual.

After many, many years, in the late 1980s, my son (I had got married, my wife is here – June) Mukti (Mukti is my son and Maya my daughter), without consulting me, without my prompting, went to Rajasthan. He went to my birthplace, and he went to find Tulsi. And he went to Acharya Tulsi and said, "I am the son of your former monk, and I have come to see my father's guru." And I did not know he was going. He just came to India and went there and discovered Acharya Tulsi for himself. And Acharya Tulsi was very surprised. And after some discussion, he asked my son, "Have you got a pen and paper?" So my son took out pen and paper, and Acharya Tulsi told him, "Write a message. Satish, I forgive you. And what you have done, what you have achieved, you have gone walking around the world, working for peace, working for the ecology, for the environment, you are continuing to be a monk without being in a robe. Come and see me. All is forgiven."

My son came to me and said, "Daddy, you have to go. Your guru wants to see you desperately. You have to go." So then I had to go. I went, actually I went twice. I went once and then again, the second time, I went with my wife June. And both times he was very welcoming and forgiving, and we reconciled.

So my mother died having reconciled with me, and my guru also passed away having reconciled with me. I am very happy that neither died without reconciliation ... Those were two very important figures in my life – my mother and my guru. And if they had died without our having reconciled, I would have felt a great sorrow in my heart, for I had a very close, personal, human, heart connection with them. So that was very good.

Grihastha ashram*

I: After such a strong training of nine years of renunciation, you left it, having been inspired by Mahatma Gandhi's autobiography. You became a householder, a family man – a *grihastha*. How do you now see this role as a *grihastha* in your pursuit of the spiritual path?

Satish: First of all, there is a difference between Jain thinking and Gandhian thinking, which is more influenced by Hindu thinking.

In Hinduism, the four stages of a man's life, *brahmacharya ashram* [*a life of celibacy, at the younger age*], *grihastha ashram* [*a family man*], *vanaprastha ashram** [*away from family and living, literally, in the forest*] and *sanyas ashram* [*a time of renunciation in service of a spiritual journey*] and are all important. If you look at our Hindu tradition, the Vaishnav* tradition, the Lords, like Krishna with Radha, Sita with Rama, Lakshmi with Narayan, Shiva with Parvati, all our tradition and our culture is of *grihastha ashram* and celebration of marriage, celebration of relationship, celebration of family, togetherness. So, from that point of view, my Jain background and upbringing was influenced more by the Hindu tradition. You can be deeply spiritual and religious as a *grihastha*. And so, I embraced that way of thinking.

As for my first marriage, when E.P. Menon [*who was an initiator of the original peace walk during the time of the Cuban missile crisis*] and I decided that we will go around the world on foot, and I went home that day and announced the news to my wife, her first reaction was, "Oh good, and I'll go with you". And we had a small baby. I phoned Menon, and Menon came, and Menon and I and Lata, we sat together. And Menon said, "With a baby you can't come. Who will look after the baby?' We are going through Muslim countries, Christian countries, communist countries, capitalist countries, deserts, mountains, we don't know what is going to happen to us. So, either Satish comes or he doesn't but you can't come with him."

She said, "If Sita can go with Rama [in Indian mythology, Lord Rama was heir to the throne but he was banished to the forest because of the stratagems of his step-mother, and his wife Sita went with him into exile], I can go with Satish, what is the problem, we are married." Menon said, "Sita did not have a baby. You have a baby, a few months old." When she learnt that neither Menon nor I thought it was a good idea that she came with us, she became angry. She said that I was being very cruel to her and to our child by going on that walk. And there was a big dilemma, a big challenge, a big paradox, a big problem. I don't know how to put it, and I have not written anything about it, but it was almost a kind of sacrifice of your marriage at the altar of some kind of conviction. Whether it was a right decision or a wrong decision, I cannot say. That was the decision.

But then Lata reconciled and she came to say goodbye at the station when we were leaving to meet Vinoba. For the time being she was reconciled to the idea. But the wound in her heart I think still remained. She thought she had been left for two years. She found another relationship too, so things didn't work out. So you can say it was a kind of sacrifice – of marriage at the altar of my peace journey, my peace pilgrimage and my work. It is very difficult to explain.

I: But I was curious about something else. I raised this question about *grihastha ashram* because apparently at first you did not want to take on the *grihastha's* role of pursuing an economic activity and supporting the family – so your in-laws did not approve of you.

Satish: What I was saying was that I would like to be a householder but not a merchant, not a businessman, and making money, because I was already inspired before marriage and was committed and dedicated to Gandhian activities and Vinoba. So my father-in-law, my mother-in-law, my brother-in-law ... all wondered what would happen to their daughter, sister, if I lived such a frugal life. What the Gandhians give you would be a pittance – bread on your plate and clothes on your body, but nothing more, they felt. So that was a bone of contention already. And on top of that I was leaving Lata behind.

One thing that made me feel a little better was that Siddharaj Dhadda, who was the president of the Sarva Seva Sangh at that time, said that what I was doing was absolutely wonderful. "Vinoba has given you blessings and I support you, you are doing a wonderful thing. You are doing Gandhian work abroad. So your salary, which Sarva Seva Sangh pays you, will continue to be paid to your wife while you are away."

That reassured me a little bit, that at least now nobody can say that I had left Lata without any support and she had to live off and be supported by her parents and brother. So Sarva Seva Sangh continued to pay my salary to Lata while I was away for two and a half years.

I: To reframe my question. Lata said you were cruel to her. From her perspective that was a very fair, reasonable comment. And if you look at it ethically, one might be tempted to argue that for a bigger right a lot of small wrongs have to be committed. But starting to do something on a base that is not right ...

Satish: You could put it that way, but I would say that for something that inspires you and you feel dedicated and convinced about and you have the courage of your convictions about, then you have to sacrifice certain personal lives and personal relationships, personal comforts and personal things. So, it is a kind of sacrifice one has to make, and this was at the altar of my conviction and at the altar of peace. I knew I had to make this sacrifice of my personal life in order to achieve this great cause of peace. At that time the idea of nuclear war was very strong. It was the height of the Cold War. There was the Soviet Union on one side and the United States on the other, and they were at loggerheads. And the whole world was tense. The scientists used to say that at any time a nuclear war or accident could happen.

I was so agitated and excited and also so inspired to do something for this grave situation the world was facing at that moment. And this is what I said to Lata, for our own child's sake I must stop nuclear weapons. We all have to do something, otherwise what kind of world will our child inherit? And that was one of the arguments that Lata did see, and in the end she came to say goodbye and reconcile, but not 100%, but she reconciled at least a little bit outwardly. So there it was: first I want to go with you, then I am angry with you, then all right I will support you as you are doing a good job for a great cause. There was ambivalence and a lot of psychological ups and downs. It was a very delicate matter, very difficult to explain.

CHAPTER 4:

Editor in London ~ The Story of *Resurgence*

Satish Kumar meets the famous economist E.F. Schumacher, author of the classic Small is Beautiful, *in England. At Schumacher's request, he ends up staying in Britain, reviving and editing* Resurgence, *a magazine on alternative, holistic, spiritual ways of living, for four decades.*

I: You told us about Schumacher asking you to stay back to run the magazine. It had run into trouble and you got it back in order. What crossed your mind when Schumacher made the offer? How did you become an ecologist? Did your Jain training have a role to play?

Satish: I met E.F. Schumacher when I went to England. He was also a Gandhian economist and was one of the associate editors of *Resurgence*. They were looking for a full-time editor. "You are Gandhian, you have all the right principles, why don't you become the editor of *Resurgence*?" he asked me. I told him I wanted to go back to India and work with the Gandhian movement.

He said, "But Satish, there are many Gandhians in India, we need one in England. Stay and make *Resurgence* a Gandhian magazine and promote peace, non-violence and ecology, spirituality and a holistic way of thinking, and spread Gandhian values through *Resurgence*."

He was very persuasive. I told him, "If I become the editor, will you write in every issue of *Resurgence*? We need somebody like you to write, to make the magazine really a strong magazine. And your article would be the backbone of the magazine." He agreed. So we had a partnership.

Schumacher was a wonderful economist, a wonderful man, a very good friend. I edited *Resurgence* for 43 years. During that time, when Schumacher died, I also established Schumacher College. Then I and my friend helped Vandana Shiva create Bija Vidyapeeth [Earth University] in India.

I came to the view that peace is not merely an absence of war. I had a long discussion with Bertrand Russell about this. Peace is a way of life. And if we want to make peace it has to begin with ourselves and then extend to people, but also entails making peace with nature.

When Schumacher invited me to edit and make *Resurgence* a Gandhian magazine, I felt that it was a good invitation, one that would give me the opportunity to broaden the idea of peace in Western thinking. In India we would admit that, naturally, peace is a way of life – *shanti, shanti*. And that peace is not simply absence of war.

But in the West, peace is very narrow. I could use the platform of *Resurgence* to grow the idea of peace and bring spirituality, social issues and ecology together, under the banner of peace. And I did that with a perfectly Gandhian approach. Gandhi is interpreted in different ways, but as I understand him, he included your personal life, your personal living and spiritual life as essential prerequisites for your political and social life. Although Gandhi was not explicit about the ecology and the environment, he demonstrated his sensitivity towards these matters in the conduct of his life. However, implicitly, when he advocates *Sarvodaya*, he is referring to the uplift of all living beings and not just human beings, as *sarva* means all, and *udaya* means uplift. He considered all life as sacred, and that would mean concern for the ecology, for the environment. And this is why I accepted the invitation from E.F. Schumacher.

I: Tell us more about *Resurgence*.

Satish: We try to say that it is a holistic magazine, which means that all subjects are interconnected. If you are to talk about politics, you have to include economics, if you include economics, you have to include ecology. If you are talking about economics and ecology you have to include the arts and culture because you cannot separate them. If you just become an economist without art and culture, then it is not good. If you just become a scientist without spirituality, it is not good, and something is lacking. So, whatever we write, we write from a multi-disciplinary perspective.

And so, in that holistic context, when we started the magazine in 1966, it was still focusing very much on peace, because at that time peace was the prominent need of the hour. But we said that peace cannot happen if organisations, nations, businesses, corporations, are too big. So 'small is beautiful' is a prerequisite for peace. The moment you become too big it becomes competitive and it becomes conflict-oriented and also bureaucratic. And it diminishes the imagination. If you are working in a big organisation you have to follow the rules of the organisation, and individual people cannot use their imagination and their creativity to make decisions.

Decisions are made at a corporate level, at a high level. And the thousands of people at the lower level just have to implement them. So, 'small is beautiful' it is, from the perspective of imagination, creativity, initiative and human fulfilment. 'Small is beautiful' was one of the most important messages that *Resurgence* carried. E.F. Schumacher was a continuous and regular contributor to every issue, and when he wrote the book *Small is Beautiful*, he incorporated in it some of the articles he wrote in *Resurgence*. And some of the ideas which he put in his book he developed in *Resurgence* first. So, small is beautiful, but not always. You can be small, and you can be ugly too.

Small countries can be exploitative. So small *should* be beautiful, not just small *is* beautiful. In order to be beautiful, you have to address, first of all, our relationship with the environment. So small is beautiful, but it should be based on a proper, sustainable and non-exploitative relationship with nature. In fact, nature is not separate from humans. So *Resurgence* promotes the idea that humans are not separate from nature. The idea of separation is the biggest problem of our time – disconnection and separation.

Resurgence also tells the story of relationship. We are all related, we are all connected, we are all interdependent. That is why one of my books is called *You are, therefore I am*. The Earth is, so I am; the sun is, so I am; the rain is, therefore I am; my parents were, therefore I am; and my teachers were, therefore I am. I am made of millions of relationships.

The modern, Western, industrial, materialist worldview is of separation. Humans are separate, then Indians and non-Indians are separate, then among Indians, Hindus are separate from Muslims and Christians and others. Then your caste* is separate, and so on. *Resurgence* upholds the value of unity of life. Unity of life does not mean uniformity. Unity of life means everything is connected but manifesting in millions of forms.

So diversity and unity can dance together. And *Resurgence* advocates diversity not as a division but as a celebration. Because if seven billion people spoke one language, had one religion, ate only one kind of food and wore only one kind of dress, that would be boring. Diversity is an outcome of evolution, evolution favours diversity, biodiversity, cultural diversity, religious diversity, linguistic diversity, truth diversity ... there is not just one truth because each of us experiences truth in our own way, so there is even truth diversity.

Diversity of every kind is very crucial in the philosophy of *Resurgence*. So, in a nutshell, *Resurgence* stands for this holistic, inter-related, interconnected, interdependent way of being. That is its basic philosophy.

Reverential Ecology, a new concept

I: How did this relate to the ideas of Arne Næss?

Satish: Arne Næss was a great friend of mine and of *Resurgence*. He was a personal friend. He developed the idea of 'deep ecology'. What he said, and it was very close to the *Resurgence* philosophy, was that we value nature not just in terms of its usefulness to humans, but nature has intrinsic value. The tree is there, the tree is good.

I: Irrespective of its usefulness?

Satish: Irrespective of human connection and human benefit. We don't preserve and conserve and respect trees because they give us oxygen, they give us fruit, shade, wood for fire – all that is fine but beside the point. We respect the tree for its own sake.

I: 'I love you for you.' Existence value?

Satish: So that is deep ecology. But *Resurgence* goes a step further, and that is what I have written in an article in one of its issues. I say that deep is good, and I totally support, and *Resurgence* totally supports, the idea of deep ecology, of the intrinsic value of nature. But that does not go far enough. We not only value nature for its own sake, but nature is sacred, it is divine. So I say, there is shallow ecology, deep ecology, and the next step is reverential ecology.

You can have a deep ecology without reverence, without a sense of the sacred. *Resurgence* embraces the idea of deep ecology, but goes further and says nature is sacred and we revere nature.

Another contributor to *Resurgence* has been James Lovelock, who invented the idea of Gaia [the Goddess who personified the Earth in Greek mythology] and has been a regular contributor. He is a good friend too. We revere Gaia, and we have been promoting the idea of Gaia.

What we say is, the old science story is that the Earth is a dead rock. James Lovelock and Gaia theory say that the Earth is a living organism, and *Resurgence* embraces the idea that the Earth is a living earth, not a dead rock. It is a living organism that is self-controlled, self-managed, self-sustaining, self-regulating ... like, climate, weather and temperature are regulated by the Earth in a self-organised way. So deep ecology and Gaia – these are the two most important philosophies, including reverential ecology, sacred earth and sacred life. These are the two big ideas which *Resurgence* has promoted and propagated.

I: Did you specifically bring this convergence as an editor, or did it evolve as contributions came in?

Satish: A bit of both because, being in the editor's chair, I try to bring all this together. There is a selection of authors and friendships I made, like James Lovelock and Arne Næss . We had a regular column by Vandana Shiva, 'Voice from the South'. She talks about the Indian perspective, agriculture, seed saving ... We must have published about forty articles by her.

I: How many columns would you have contributed?

Satish: Oh, that would be very difficult to count, in forty-three years I must have written hundreds. They are a bit dated. But some of those ideas have emerged in different forms in my books. I have published six. *Resurgence* was also instrumental in establishing Schumacher College.

I: Not the other way around? *Resurgence* got the college going?

Satish: Yes. The college opened in 1991, and *Resurgence* started in 1966, and so is much older. *Resurgence* created Schumacher College.

I: *Resurgence* appears to have been quite the hub around which some of the best-known names in ecology and allied subjects communed.

Satish: *Resurgence*'s 50th anniversary (celebrated in 2016) had many mainstream speakers, including Prince Charles, Lord David Putnam, and the deans of the University of Cambridge and three colleges, and the editor-in-chief of the *Guardian*, who is now the dean of one of the colleges at Oxford. An Oxford College, Worcester College, hosted it, so it was a mainstream discussion and debate.

There were three days of events and nearly a thousand people came, and there were 50 speakers, many of them quite mainstream. They all debated ecology, spirituality, global warming, climate change, organic farming. Then we organise the *Resurgence* Festival of Wellbeing annually. There again we have a public debate on how to shift our focus from economic growth to growth and wellbeing. Because the purpose of economic growth should be wellbeing. But people don't think about wellbeing, they only talk about economic growth as GDP growth. It is usually attended by 300 to 400 people.

Then we have monthly *Resurgence* talks in London, given by environmentalists, thinkers, and so on. Many from the mainstream attend. So those are the kinds of events we organise at Schumacher College.

Resurgence was also instrumental in establishing a publishing house called Green Books, which is now headquartered and run as an independent company in Cambridge, England.

I: Is *Resurgence* – or you, personally – associated with the International Society for Ecological Economics?

Satish: Herman Daley, who co-founded the Society, and others associated with it have contributed articles to *Resurgence* ... we are connected with the Society informally. Herman Daley, particularly, contributed many articles to the magazine. He is a great, wonderful economist. Then there was David Orr who contributed articles regularly to *Resurgence*. So, a number of ecological economists have contributed articles. They are all very close to Schumacherian economics, contributing to *Resurgence* and supporting it.

I: Has anything published in *Resurgence* caused controversy?

As far as controversial writing is concerned, everything we print in *Resurgence* is very controversial in terms of mainstream society. The *Guardian* newspaper has called *Resurgence* the "artistic and spiritual flagship of the green movement". I have appeared in the *Guardian* a number of times, and many of our contributors, such as Jonathan Porritt or Caroline Lucas, are from the political world. Caroline Lucas is a Green MP and she is a contributor to *Resurgence*. Everything that we were writing from 1966 to the late 1960s and 1970s has been ahead of its time. We wrote about renewable energy. Nobody was writing about renewable energy. We are always opposed to nuclear power, and that is very controversial because mainstream society, government and, generally speaking, people, are supporting nuclear power. We say nuclear power is the beginning of nuclear weapons ... (they are at) a similar sort of energy level.

Even promoting Gaia was controversial, because the academic world, particularly people like Richard Dawkins, pooh-poohed Gaia Theory. They are Oxford academics; they challenged and did not accept the theory. But *Resurgence* promoted it. So, the things that *Resurgence* publishes are often very controversial. Even *Small is Beautiful* is very controversial. People want to grow bigger and bigger – they want bigger hospitals, bigger schools, bigger economy, bigger GDP, bigger nations, everything bigger. It is a little like Gandhian thinking being controversial in India.

I: How many articles would Schumacher have contributed? Did he begin to write only after you joined?

Satish: Thirty-five articles. No, he was writing before that. He was one of the editors, but he was not writing regularly. His articles have been published in a collection called *This I Believe*, by Green Books.

I: As *Resurgence* is based in the UK, do you see any continuity in thinking from John Ruskin, Thomas Carlyle, Edward Carpenter and our friend who wrote *The Indian Village*?

Satish: Yes, absolutely. John Ruskin had been one of the mentors of *Resurgence*, and also Schumacher, not so much Carlyle and Carpenter, but some others. If you look at *Resurgence*, we have always carried an article under the series called 'Pioneers', and we published a book, *One Hundred Visionaries*, which includes thinkers like Henry D. Thoreau, John Ruskin, Aldo Leopold, author of *A Sand County Almanac*, and many ecologists and environmentalists. Also featured are Gandhi, Vinoba, Aseem Shrivastava and Fritjof Capra. Yes, I met many of them.

I: Capra was visiting faculty at Schumacher College?

Satish: Yes, many times, and he has been a good friend contributing to *Resurgence* many times. David Orr was regular faculty, Herman Daley also. Thomas Berry ... have you heard of him and Wendell Berry? He wrote a book called *The Unsettling of America: Culture and Agriculture*. And Thomas Berry wrote a book, *The Dream of the Earth*. We have presented in *Resurgence* many wonderful thinkers.

Chapter 5:

Who am I?

The Covid-19 pandemic and the economic downturn brought a lot of pain but also triggered some new thinking. People feel lost and scared. As the busyness of daily life slowed down for a while, new questions about the way we live and who we are came to the fore.

Almost all religions evolved not to burden people with identities, but to liberate them from all labels. The inquiry goes deeper not into the wide world but into the self. Who am I – that is the ultimate question that has been asked and probed by mystics and people of wisdom over millennia. Modern practice seemed to have forgotten that question, says Satish Kumar.

Q. How do you see yourself or describe yourself today?

Satish: Whatever words you use, they become a label. 'I am an Indian' is a label, 'I am Satish Kumar' is a label. 'I am Gandhian' is a label. 'I was born a Jain' another label. Labels narrow you down. Language is a very tricky business – it separates, and dualism comes in. Ultimately, we have to rise above labels and consider ourselves as living beings, human beings. But even 'human being' is a label because it separates you from other living beings. We are actually made of earth, air, fire, water, space and consciousness.

These elements are common to all of us, whether you are Indian, American, Russian or Chinese; or Hindu, Muslim or Christian; or Gandhian, socialist, communist or capitalist. Beyond all those labels, we are made of the same things —consciousness, spirit and the five elements.

For the sake of convenience, you can use labels. You can put any label you like on me. Because I was with Vinoba for many years, I was a Sarvodayee. As I edited a journal of his *bhoodan** movement, I was also a little of a journalist. I edited *Resurgence*, promoting Gandhian values. Eventually I was honoured by the Jamnalal Bajaj award [a well-known award in India honouring public work based on Gandhian principles] for promoting Gandhian values abroad. You can put the label of Gandhian on me, but ultimately it is a label.

I don't like to say that I am carrying on Gandhi's work or something, for who can claim such a thing? So I can only say that I am very inspired by Gandhi, I am very influenced by Gandhi. But I am carrying *my* heart. I can only do what I feel and believe, and go by my convictions.

Q. If you don't have anything to do with the labels; then what do you see? Many people would say they feel lost. What do you have to tell them?

Satish: When you go beyond the labels you have to see the person you are talking to at that moment. How Satish Kumar was even yesterday or last year is not what he is today; and what he will be tomorrow, next year or in five years, is not the same Satish Kumar. We are changing all the time.

So there is no fixed identity. When we assume a fixed identity, we become rigid, we become dogmatic, we become almost fundamentalist. I am what I appear to you now at this moment, fresh and spontaneous, and whatever I speak is improvisation. There is nothing fixed from the past. I try to be a dynamic, moving, changing pilgrim on a journey, like a river always flowing. It is not the same water which you see now that you will see another two or five minutes later. It is fresh water, but the same river.

So (I would tell confused people), everybody's identity is always dynamic. Rudolph Steiner says that in seven years you change completely. You don't have anything of the past, even though your facial expressions and facial appearance may be similar (to what was before), you are not the same. So, 'who am I?' is a big question, and the moment you start saying 'I am not this, I am not that', that is the only answer. In the Vedic tradition, we say '*neti, neti, neti*', not this, not that, neither this nor that. In Buddhist terminology, it is *shoonyata*, emptiness. We are empty of any kind of fixed identity. We are always dynamic, moving, changing, transforming. So, who am I? – I am pure spirit. My identity is not fixed. It is dynamic, it's not rigid.

I: You say this with a lot of sparkle in your eyes.

Satish: (Laughs) That is the living quality of human beings. In our eyes, in our face, we have a smile, we have a sparkle, and the moment we keep that freshness, the moment we celebrate that freshness and are with it, then we are free. Freedom is not something to be achieved tomorrow or next year or in later life or in the next life. Freedom happens the moment you appreciate your dynamic and not rigid state. You are free, a free spirit.

We are all everything

And what happens in our society is that our education, or our religion, or our politics, or our jobs, try to fix us, and all spontaneity and improvisation disappears. And we try to say, you are now a lawyer, you are a doctor, you are a teacher, an accountant, an engineer, a politician, an economist. We put ourselves in compartments. So, when I am a doctor, I am not a teacher; and when I am a teacher, I am not a lawyer, and when I am a lawyer, I am not an accountant. But we are, everybody, all of these. When I am keeping my accounts, I am an accountant. When I am putting some medicine on my hurt toe, I am a doctor; and when I am teaching or giving a talk, I am a teacher. We are all, in one body, everything. We don't have to compartmentalise and specialise in one direction. So that is how you can keep yourself fresh and have a sparkle in your eyes.

I: Attachment to identities is leading to violence everywhere. How do you explain non-violence to young people, coming from your Jain and Gandhian background?

Satish: Actually, Mahatma Gandhi was influenced a lot by the Jain idea of non-violence. One of his teachers was Shrimad Rajchandra, who was a merchant, but he was a tremendously simple and frugal person. [*"Shrimadji shaped Gandhiji's ideas and guided his beliefs. He played a pivotal role in the making of the Mahatma, on the basis of which Gandhiji achieved India's independence and inspired generations. Their legacies continue to offer new paradigms to global peace and human progress", according to the Shrimad Rajchandra Mission.*] The Gandhian concept of non-violence, which is so broad and all-encompassing, all inclusive, is coming from a Jain tradition to some extent, and particularly from Shrimad Rajchandra. Also, Gandhi was very inclusive; he was also influenced by Tolstoy, Henry D. Thoreau, John Ruskin – so there were many great influences on him. He was very humble and receptive. He would learn from any quarter, anywhere.

The idea of Jain non-violence is that you are never going to be completely non-violent but you can minimise harm, and particularly, intention. Do no harm with intention. If your intention is pure, then your action will be pure, so minimise your actions, and thereby you become vegetarian or you don't use leather or don't consume honey or animal products. Minimise your violence and you will have a minimal impact on the environment. I think this is where Mahatma Gandhi got his idea of non-violence. There is enough in the world for everybody's need but not for everybody's greed. That is the Jain idea of *aparigraha**, that if you remain restrained and limit the use of the resources of the earth then there is abundance in nature. That was the Jain influence on Gandhi's philosophy.

I: How is non-violence related to *moksha*?*

Satish: *Mukta** [*generally, being free of worldly attachments, and moksha is being free of the cycle of life and death, but they are used interchangeably by many, including Satish in this conversation*] is being detached and liberated internally. If you are inflicting violence on others for your own benefit and comfort, for your convenience, for your own wealth, for yourself, the moment you are self-centred, self-absorbed and self-conscious, then you cannot be liberated. To be liberated, you have to let go of your self-centred and self-promotional attitude. When you do that, you have to be kind. This is where Jains go very far, really far. Hindus don't go that far. Jains don't eat onion or garlic, because that would mean removing the plant and disturbing the soil. Jains are not, in principle, allowed to do mining, etc. Although Jain merchants deal in diamonds, they are not allowed to do mining, traditionally, though many Jains don't follow all this anymore. Many Jains are just lapsed Jains, they have become ritualistic, rather than authentic.

I: That is true of people of all religions, isn't it?

Satish: The idea was that in order to liberate yourself, you have to be compassionate and kind to all living beings and not be self-centred and use other beings for your own personal benefit, comfort, convenience and so on. You don't engage in any *arambh** [execution of activity] or *samarambh** [preparation for activity], those are the words you use. They refer to unnecessary activities. So, minimise your unnecessary impact on planet Earth and maximise your attention and time on your meditation, chanting, studying, singing, poetry, study of philosophy. In that way you are liberating your inner self and that leads to *moksha*. That is the connection. *Moksha* is liberation from all attachments, from all self-absorption and self-centredness.

I: And would you tell young people that they can do that even when they are not in the *sanyasa* – renunciation – mode?

Satish: In the Jain tradition, they say you ultimately take *sanyasa*. [*You leave behind everything else, possessions and family, when you decide to follow the* *path of renunciation.*] But the Hindu tradition says you can be a *sanyasi* even in *grihastha ashram.* [You can set out on the spiritual path even while you are a family man.] I like that Hindu idea, because I feel that Hindus are more celebratory. They celebrate the gifts of life with frugality and simplicity. So it is that in the Hindu tradition, you have all the great dance forms like Bharatanatyam* and Kathakali*, and you have good music, Karnatic music* and many other types of beautiful music, and bhajans and kirtans*. There is music, poetry, dance, architecture, temples ... In all these, the sense of beauty is very strong among the Hindus, but the Jains are austere. Even my guru, Acharya Tulsi ... he was so austere. We do not have image worship and we don't have temples, as by building temples you are getting into violence.

I: No *derasar* (as the Jain place of worship is known)?

Satish: The Terapanthi [a sect of Jainism] have no *derasar*, because you are still engaging in using nature. Minimise. Only one set of spare clothes and one begging bowl, and keep wandering – so simple.

I: And you stay in someone's house?

Satish: You stay in someone's house for a day or two. And during *chaturmas** you stay in some *dharmashala* [rest house for travellers, especially pilgrims]. You don't disturb anybody. So, Jains go to the extreme path of reducing their impact on environment, on nature, on other people.

I: There are also the naked *sadhus*.

Satish: Yes, that is even more extreme. They are the Digambar *sadhus*. You can see them even today. There are about 70 to 80 Digambar monks in India.

I: And they do not wear anything because clothes also involve violence?

Satish: They are possessions. You have to minimise your possessions, and more important, minimise or eliminate your inner possessions, which are ego, pride and greed. When you are free of those, then you are liberated.

I: And you would say you are also on the path to *moksha*?

Satish: *Moksha* is very difficult to define. Many great philosophers, from Radhakrishnan to Ramana Maharshi, including Gandhi and Vinoba, have tried to define it. For me, *moksha* is not a static state, not a fixed state. The moment you are free of ego, pride, possessions, inner and outer, and you are detached, and you are spontaneous and living in the moment and celebrating *ananda* [joy], *sat-chit-ananda* [truth, consciousness, bliss; the bliss that comes from consciousness of the truth], that is the state of *moksha*. But it is not such that you have reached *moksha*, and then nothing else ever happens. You could fluctuate, and you could be in a state of *nirvana**, a state of *moksha**, completely free, and suddenly some wave* comes, and you can be not in a state of *moksha*. So that is one approach.

The other, according to the Jains, is when after death you are in *moksha* and you don't return to the cycle of birth and death. That is another interpretation. But I don't go too much into that – rebirth and *moksha* after birth. *Moksha* in that state would be like this house. There is space. If you remove the space in the house, you remove the walls, then this space which is now in the room has been liberated from the walls and has become part of the larger space outside. In the same way, our spirit is part of that consciousness, and our body is limited by consciousness. If the body is gone and you are so pure you don't take a next body, you are part of consciousness. So that pure consciousness is the state of *moksha*. That is one understanding of pure consciousness.

You don't have to die for *moksha*

But even when you are in your body you can still be in a state of keeping the doors and windows open. Fresh air is coming in, and you are not really too stuffy, stagnant or fixed. You have an open heart, an open mind. You are liberated and not prejudiced and not fixed to your identities of family, nationality, religion. You are not fixed to your ideas, your ideology, your values and views. There is a place beyond right and wrong, beyond intellectual thinking and feelings and ideas, and that's where *moksha* is. But we deal mainly with the realm of ideas, thinking, labels, and so on, and we are part of the *samsara** [the material world]. But when we are beyond that and transcend all concepts and all ideas, then we are in the state of *moksha*. So, in this life if you can reach that stage, you reach *moksha*.

The Jain idea of *moksha* is that with your karma disappearing, you don't build any more walls, you don't come to live in any more bodies. It is your karma which brings you back. Karma is our desire, our need to build a house, to build walls – that is our desire. So as long as we have desires, we come back. The moment you are free of desires, you don't need to come back. Your karma has gone, disappeared. The *Bhagavad Gita**

would say that if you act without desire for the fruit of your action, then you will not be bound by the karma of your action. Because desire is the glue that sticks karma on you. When there is no desire, then action is just action, it has no consequence. In that case, it is only a living process: there is no consequence and there is no karma. Karma is connected with desires.

I: How does one convey the message particularly to Western audiences in today's context that material requirements must be minimised for good living and for attaining higher forms of awareness?

Satish: Even in Western civilisation, there are spiritual people. And Gandhi was not talking about them. Gandhi was talking about the Western civilisation that was focused on the industrial and material world, not about people like St Francis. Gandhi was very much influenced by people like Tolstoy, Thoreau, Bernard Shaw, and by Quakers, Christians and others from the West. What he was talking about was Western *industrial* civilisation. Even Eastern civilisation is not perfect, there are many materialists, atheists, *nastiks* [atheists], and so on.

When Gandhi talked about *swaraj* [which calls for a decentralised, small-scale, self-organised, self-managed local system of governance and consumption], he was using it as a metaphor. It was a way of explaining the concept. The so-called Western civilisation, which Gandhi criticised, is dominating the entire world. It is no longer just the West which is that way. China is the same, India is going down the same path more and more, and so too the African and South American countries, and Australia. The whole world is now under the tsunami of industrial, materialistic, consumer-oriented Western civilisation.

I: Therefore, are we living in a bubble or deluding ourselves when we try to strike an alternative path and think the world can change?

Satish: The answer to this civilisation is to create a new paradigm, which may be at the moment small in scale. A minority of people are promoting this new paradigm of thinking, which is more holistic, more spiritual, more ecological. Western civilisation and this modern world are only 200 or 300 years old. It is only a blink of an eye in the geological scale of time. This will pass, and what has been created by humans can be changed and will be changed by humans. Therefore, the work of Mahatma Gandhi, the work of Schumacher, Vandana Shiva, myself, Wangari Maathai (the Kenyan activist who in 2004 became the first African woman to win the Nobel Peace Prize), and many spiritual, ecological, holistic people, is to keep the candle burning. When the moment comes, when people have seen the consequences of this materialistic, consumerist culture which is creating a polluted atmosphere, polluted water, no air to breathe, no good, right food to eat, no relationships left, no humanity left, we will wake up. What have we done? A new way of ecological restraint, a spiritual paradigm, will emerge again. That is the hope, and one has to live with hope, because without hope you don't act.

Waiting is a virtue

Mahatma Gandhi said he could wait for a hundred years before we got independence; he hoped that people would rise and appreciate the importance of *swaraj**. Therefore, time is not a problem; I will act in the right way. So, we – Vandana Shiva, myself, Vinoba Bhave – also say that time is not a problem. If it happens today or tomorrow, in our lifetime or in the lifetime of our children or grandchildren, it doesn't matter. We will pursue the path which is more eternal, more enduring, more lasting, more beautiful, more satisfying, more joyful. We will keep that little candle burning and protect it and shade it so that no wind blows it out. This civilisation is not here forever and we cannot predict how long it will last. But if our conviction and our inner voice tell us that we must keep the candle of Gandhian thinking alive, then we must keep it so, whatever the consequences, whatever the results.

I: Do you think there will be a 'great turning' of human consciousness?

Satish: That is the kind of hope we harbour, and with that hope we act.

I: Do you think it is far away, or close?

Satish: I think it is getting closer. Even in China there is a new move. They are inviting me to go to China and there are people coming to Schumacher College from China. They are saying we have to create an ecological civilisation. This kind of industrial, urban, materialistic, consumer culture that China is following is not going to last. It will destroy our people. Our communities will be destroyed, humanity will be destroyed. So even China is awakening, which is a kind of communist, atheist, non-religious, non-spiritual country, or at least that is the ruling paradigm. If this is happening even in China, then I think it will happen in India, and in the West people are waking up as well. So, one lives in hope.

CHAPTER 6:

Schumacher College

Where the syllabus mandates falling in love

Apart from editing an international sustainability journal for more than four unbroken decades, an extraordinary achievement for a former monk with no university education, Satish Kumar also co-founded Schumacher College in England, a respected institute for ecological studies. This is an unusual institution with an unusual founder that teaches ecology in an unusual way – making students participate in an alternative way of living. It is a vegetarian college that grows a lot of its food on campus, where everyday chores including toilet cleaning, in the Gandhian spirit, are a part of the learning.

I: Tell us about your experience of establishing the college.

Satish: First of all, Schumacher College has, can I say, exceeded my expectations. When we were starting the college and I got support from the Trustees of Dartington, one of the trustees said, "Satish, this is too idealistic, it is not going to last. It may last three to five years, that's it. It's not a very practical project." People were very pessimistic about the future of the college, but 26 years later, the college is flourishing, and we have more people wanting to join than we have accommodation for.

Secondly, at Schumacher College we try to keep a free spirit. We teach holistic thinking, soil, soul, society, holistic science, Gaia, deep ecology, the biocentric world view, spiritual ecology, reverence ecology, holistic design – we teach all these things. But most important is the way we live and the way we share – through communal living, everybody participating in cooking, cleaning, gardening, washing up. Living with each other and living in a community is the biggest test, because in Schumacher College we have people from different religions and cultures, speaking different languages, all coming together.

They are Brazilian, French, German, Indian, African, somebody from Ethiopia, from the Middle East ... all have to live together. You need a big heart and you need to be tolerant of each other for that. It is a kind of experiment as to how society, humanity, can live together, with diversity and differences, yet working together. That, I think, is the biggest accomplishment of Schumacher College, that we have the harmonious living together of many cultures, everybody living, working and studying together.

I often say, jokingly but half seriously, that we got you here to study holistic science, economics of transition, and many other subjects, but the real purpose is to get you to fall in love. I say to them, fall in love with each other, fall in love with life and wisdom. Fall in love with yourself, appreciate yourself. That is the real purpose of Schumacher College. But if we say to them that we are inviting them to come here to fall in love, they won't come.

They would be a bit scared. Or they would say, "Why should I pay hundreds of pounds to go there to fall in love?" So we have to say that you are coming to learn holistic science, or something else, but actually it is all a metaphor. Really, we want you to fall in love with life. And when you are in love with life, holistic science, ecology and environment, economics and everything will fall into place. Love is the mother of all virtues. If you have love in your heart, you will have peace, generosity, kindness, compassion, caring, sharing and service. Everything will flow out of love. So, the purpose of Schumacher College, ultimately, is to invite people to experience that love, to share that love and fall in love. Literally, a lot of people do fall in love and get married there.

Three kinds of love

In the Greek language, there are three words for 'love' – *agape, philia* and *eros*, and we want our Schumacher students to have all three loves. *Agape* is the love of brothers, sisters, mothers, fathers, friends and neighbours, you can call it brotherly love, sisterly love. Then there is *philia*, which is the love of ideas, vision and values, language, philology, philosophy, wisdom, philanthropy, humanity – not one or two people but humanity as a whole. And *eros* is erotic love. How wonderful it is to have another person to embrace in your arms, to have the warmth of his body in bed, how beautiful it is to kiss each other. Erotic love, romantic love, has inspired many great poets, painters, artists. We were in Ghanerao, a village in the state of Rajasthan in India, where there is the Bhakti movement. Bhakti means divine love. For the Sufis and for the people of the Bhakti movement, God comes and appears as the beloved. So, erotic love is beautiful, we all fall in love, especially when we are young, but erotic love is part of *philia* and part of *agape*, and part of divine love, Bhakti. If you can have that big vision of love, then love is not a wishy washy, flaky idea. It is a real thing. It is the mother of all virtues. Therefore, I say to people in Schumacher College, we have invited you to fall in love with life, and that is a very broad meaning of love, one including erotic love.

I: How can Schumacher College relate to the English type of living? I have lived in England and I don't see England as a country of love. I see it as a country of many beautiful things, I don't see it as a country of love.

Satish: There is not one England, there are many Englands. In England you have William Blake – he was a poet of love and imagination. You have in England many people who are organic farmers ... communities producing beautiful music, beautiful work. So, England is not only what we see as a superficial overview of business, industry, banks, government, Mrs Theresa May [British Prime Minister from 2016-2019] and Brexit and all the things you see in the media. There is another England, and also very beautiful. I walked around Britain. I went around walking for four months, 2,000 miles. I walked every day, and I walked without any money in my pocket. Every day I found people giving me hospitality and love. People, families I had never met before, strangers ... giving hospitality. They would say, "Oh, you are a pilgrim, come. Where are the pilgrims nowadays? We don't find any pilgrims. Come, stay with us. Have tea, have coffee, have a bed." England is not only what you read and see superficially. I have lived in England now for 45 years. I have seen England differently from Brexit and the media, even the BBC. That's a different England.

There is love everywhere

I think there is a lot of love in England. And it was an English trust that gave us the building and the money to create Schumacher College, even though one of them said we might last for just four or five years, but at least he gave us a chance for four or five years. And I said to him, "Michael, it is better to start and do something and fail, rather than not try something at all." And he said, all right, try, and he gave his blessings. And it was in England that Rabindranath Tagore said to Leonard and Dorothy Elmhirst, "Go and create Dartington Hall". And they bought 1,000 acres under the Dartington Hall Trust. So there are many good things in England. We have to embrace them and celebrate them, then we can critique Brexit and the media and things which are not so good.

In India it is the same. There is a lot of love, culture, the Sanskrit language; many people are very hospitable, in rural India especially. But when you go to Mumbai and see government and business and Ambani [Mukesh Ambani is a well-known Indian industrialist who lives in an opulent skyscraper mansion in Mumbai] and big pollution and waste, that's not the India that I want to see. There are two Indias: an India of imagination, of love, and also the India of waste, pollution and politics. I embrace the first India and ignore or critique this mainstream India.

I was invited to speak at the London School of Economics. I asked them, "Can you please tell me where your department for ecology is?" And the professor said, "What do you mean? We are a school of economics. We don't teach ecology. We have some courses within the economics department, like development, sustainability, environment; but we don't teach ecology as such." I said, "I am sorry to challenge or question, but you are a professor. The words ecology and economy come from the Greek words, *oikos, logos* and *nomos. Oikos* means planet home in the wisdom of the Greek philosophers. Home is not only where you have your bathroom and bedroom and kitchen, but the entire planet is your home. *Logos* means knowledge, like logic. So, knowing your planet is ecology – how everything works together, how everything goes in harmony and is interrelated – that is ecology, knowledge of your home. And then *nomos* means management. So, when you know it, then you manage it. But if you don't know what you are managing, how are you going to manage it? You are sending these thousands of graduates all over the world (because LSE is a world-renowned university) and they are managing something they don't know."

No wonder the world's economy is in a mess, because they don't know what they are managing. You need to teach everybody ecology and economy together, and I even suggested that they should change the name of their university and call it LSEE, London School of Ecology and Economics. You will be the world leader. But the professor said that it was not in her hands, and she took it with a bit of humour. But the problem with our university system is that they are part of the problem, not part of the solution.

Money-nomy

They are educating and teaching young people to exploit the natural world and also humans. And it is not about ecology nor about economy, it is about money-nomy, money-making. Everything has turned into a commodity to make money with.

So, education should make money; medicine, business, politics and everything should make money. Money is the controlling factor, and that is the biggest problem with our education. Young people are being trained to work in big companies, or in government, bureaucracy, business, and they are all very destructive. They are polluting and wasting and they are full of greed, controlled by money. So, the education of modern times is part of the problem and not part of the solution. Everybody talks about education, but what is education? What we are giving is not really education – it is a kind of brainwashing and job seeking.

The purpose of education is not to look for a job

Universities produce millions of graduates around the world. Someone has to give them a job – government, business or industry. That is not right. I say, when I teach at Schumacher College (we created Schumacher College for a different kind of education), "When you have finished at Schumacher College, don't go and look for a job, but create your own eco-entrepreneurship, social entrepreneurship, by which your job should be in harmony with the natural world, the social world, and in harmony with your own satisfaction, fulfilment and joy. Therefore, if you look for a job with a big company, just for salary, so that you can have a lot of material goods and consumer goods and possessions, that is not the purpose of education." I think education needs a complete revolution. Education, the university system, the school system at the moment, disempowers people, disenfranchises people. They come out of university, they can just think – there is head, but no heart and no hands. So, education should be a combination of head, heart and hands, these three words should go together. I think we need a big revolution, and I think Gujarat Vidyapith [an institution in India founded by Gandhi in 1920 and now a university offering, among other subjects, Gandhian Studies and Rural Management] can renew and revive, and lead a new kind of education.

And if the government says that you have to follow the rules, otherwise you will not get money, say, "Go away, we will not take your money. Either you give money for what we are doing, or we won't take your money." Be courageous and let them withdraw your money and then let ordinary people and the students themselves and philanthropists, let them support. Schumacher College is completely supported by philanthropists and students. We do not take a single penny from the government. Even if the government wants to give us money, we say, "No, thank you. We don't want to be controlled by you." So, Gujarat Vidyapith, particularly, started by Mahatma Gandhi, can be a shining example for the whole world to see that people coming out of the university are self-reliant, they can make, they can cook, they can garden, grow food, like at Schumacher College.

Everyone their own maid

At Schumacher College, there is a new model of education. Everyone must participate in cooking, gardening, cleaning – there are no staff to do this. Even I cook. For twenty-six years, I have been cooking there, every week.

And I say, if there is a meeting, have it before cooking time or after cooking time, but not between 4.30 and 6.30p.m., because that is my cooking time and I don't want to have any meeting at that time. Every member of the staff participates in cooking. The Director of Schumacher College also does the washing up. There is no point in being a Gandhian university and then having staff to do the washing up. We must do our own washing up. Schumacher College is a Gandhian college, so we adopted a Gandhian system. As Mahatma Gandhi did everything, so we should do everything.

This is also what I say about Harijans* [literally 'children of God', the name Gandhi gave to the lower castes*] and Dalits* [The reformer Mahatma Jyotirao Phule (1826-1890), is thought to have first used the term to describe the outcastes and untouchables in India.] If we want to remove the stigma of being low caste, Harijan or Dalit, we have to do – and give dignity to – all these things like cleaning the toilet. What's the problem? If you are going to use the toilet to defecate, why get somebody else to clean it? That is the Schumacher principle. We have created a college as an alternative to mainstream education, because mainstream education is exploitative, and trains students to exploit and be selfish. They train you for personal success, whereas our education is not for your personal success. Your success will come when you serve others; planet Earth, humanity and the poor; you serve for the sense of service. Rabindranath Tagore said, "When you have a sense of service, you get joy". So that is the education model I want to see.

I: How do you introduce spirituality to students of science, and convince them that they too need to know a bit of spirituality?

Satish: For example, in every science and technology school, such as IIT and MIT, and universities, you need to teach science along with ecology and ethics, and the questioning of why we are doing science and what will be the effect of this science and technology on humans and on planet Earth. Those questions must be linked with the development of science and technology, with computers, cars, nuclear energy, weapons, everything. Whenever scientists embark on research, they should think about why they are doing it and what its impact will be on humans, nature and the environment. Those are ethical and spiritual questions to be asked in the course of their study. They must meditatively and mindfully research, and promise, as a doctor takes an oath, that they will not do research that is harmful to nature or humans. Then science and technology would have a spiritual dimension, and I will support that kind of research in science and technology.

I: Even if that means you don't research what what is within your reach?

Satish: Yes, absolutely. If it is going to have harmful effects on humans or the planet or nature, then even if it can be done, you must not do it because your commitment is to the wellbeing and integrity of human life and nature. That should not be damaged. A scientist will not make nuclear weapons if he has spiritual values.

I: There is the problem of success too. Using fossil fuels was not a problem till it became so widespread, because it was so successful.

Satish: It would not have become so large if we were driven by spiritual values. Fossil fuel is promoting consumerism, facilitating production.

I: But you see that only in hindsight, you wouldn't have known when you were digging the first well.

Satish: Gandhi saw it in the 1920s. In 1909, even earlier, many others saw it. So it was not seen only in hindsight. At the outset it was recognised by people who used their wisdom and values and were practising non-violence.

I: They were dubbed anti-science.

Satish: Vinoba always talked about science as an important aspect. But science without non-violence, without truth, without *aparigraha** can go astray, can lead us astray. So, science must accompany the principle of non-violence – towards humans, nature and towards yourself. The means and ends must be congruent. If you are pursuing noble ends with foul means, they are not worth pursuing.

I: Then you have 'Animal Farm'.

Satish: Exactly. Noble ends must be pursued by noble means. So, all science and technology MUST be – this is a very strong statement – in congruence with the principles of non-violence, ecology, sustainability, authenticity and truth. If it is not, then science alone is not enough. Science is a useful tool, like a knife. If you don't understand the principle of *how* to use the knife, and then *why* to use it, you can cut somebody's throat. That is not the purpose of the knife. I am not blaming the knife. I am blaming the people who do not understand that a knife is made for chopping vegetables and not for cutting the throats of people. In the same way, science is like a knife, it is made to serve humanity and nature through better means than we had before, rather than cut the throats of people. So, if science is used for a violent purpose, it would be misuse of science.

I: With your life-time experience, how do you define sustainability, and what would you consider non-negotiable and where would you be willing to consider trade-offs?

Satish: According to me, nature can sustain – not the way business can be sustained – but in ways that are possible within the limits of nature itself and our planet. If you go on depending on fossil fuel, for example, which is a limited resource, in the end it is not sustainable. To go on using it, however much profit you make, your business is sustained for 50 or 100 years, but the economy of nature, the economy of the Earth, is not meant to run only for a few hundred years, it is for millennia. So, we have to sustain an economy for millions of years, as a cyclical economy, which is nature's economy. Our modern economy, which is unsustainable, is a linear economy. You take, you use and you throw away. So oceans are full of plastic. Landfills are full of greenhouse gases, generating waste. This linear economy is not sustainable from the point of view of nature. Nature has to have a cyclical economy. Whatever you take from nature must go back to nature. If it does not, if it is not being reabsorbed, renewed and regenerated, then that is unsustainable. It is from that point of view that I use the word sustainability. But this word is now being misused and hijacked, like science is misused. Business is sustainable in a different way.

I: '*Vandra na haathma astro*' – a Gujarati expression.

Satish: Yes, a knife in the hands of a monkey! I understand Gujarati.

CHAPTER 7:

How We Lost True Confidence

The edifice of modern education has been built on the premise that one is not good enough, says Satish Kumar. The yardstick of success today is scoring better in exams, earning more in life, rising up the corporate ladder, ticking off the standard milestones of life ... all this has made modern man deeply discontented, and underconfident. Whatever he achieves is not enough, he is afraid others will overtake him, life will overtake him. His life is dry and joyless, and he hates himself more than anything else, and as a result hates others, too. Acceptance and love, of both oneself and others, are the two key antidotes to this problem, he says.

I: For those of us who make efforts to do something different, we find that this is not so easy. We are overwhelmed with information, and sometimes we feel we are not good enough. Then we feel we are never doing as much as we could or should. All this can be so wearying.

Satish: Yes, there is a kind of Western education, or modern education, which has come to India too. And that is to be discontented at every moment. I am not good enough because my parents said I am not good enough. Your teachers said, this essay is not good enough, this exam result is not good enough. You are not first, you are second or third in your class, you only get 70% marks, not 100%, and you are not good enough.

You have been conditioned to think that you are not good enough, so you say to yourself, "Whatever I do is never good enough". This comparing and contrasting is part of modern education.

If you want to be free of this, then you must accept yourself, love yourself, be compassionate towards yourself, be kind to yourself.

I: How do we know the difference between loving ourselves and being selfish?

Satish: Loving yourself is not being selfish. Unless you feed yourself, how are you going to feed somebody else? Unless you love yourself, how are you going to love somebody else? The Gandhian way is to be yourself, whoever you are, and to accept yourself as you are, not condemning yourself. You do not say, "I want to be like Gandhi, or Shakespeare or Neruda, like Mother Teresa, I want to be famous."

Never compare yourself; be yourself. A mango doesn't say, I want to be like the apple, and the apple doesn't say I want to be like a mango. There are sour fruits, sweet fruits, we need everybody and everything. So, you are good as you are.

Be yourself, you are good

Say to yourself, "I am good as I am, and now I am going to radiate my goodness, like a heater radiates heat and warms everybody. I will radiate who I am." If you are a dancer, be a dancer; if you are a singer, be a singer; if you are a writer, be a writer; if you are a cook, be a cook; if you are a gardener, be a gardener. Whatever is your interest, be that, be yourself. And you are very good.

You are unique. There is no-one else like you in the whole world. There are seven billion people but no-one like you. Every person is unique, special, a special gift to the world. You are a gift to the world. Have that self-confidence, self-love and self-compassion. Say, "I will serve to the best of my ability." That's all you need to say to yourself. "I will do whatever I can, whatever ability I have."

Everybody is good in themselves. This is the Gandhian principle. Gandhi said, be yourself. Don't try to copy somebody else. Don't try to compare or contrast yourself with somebody else. You are a unique, special, particular gift to the world. Be that gift. And we should celebrate everybody. We celebrate and love everybody as they are, the way we celebrate the grass as the grass is and the tree as the tree is. We have to appreciate and celebrate everybody, love everybody. Love is the landscape of life. Through love, everybody loving himself/herself and others as they are, we can live a good life.

Things do not work out as you expect. So free yourself from expectations, accept yourself and accept others and then participate (in life). The process of transformation comes from participation (in life).

We participate in discussion and this discussion will help in transformation. You participate in cooking and the food is transformed, the raw food is transformed. There should be no judgement; we do not say rice is better than wheat or wheat is better than millet, or millet is better than corn. We participate in making food and we celebrate. Participation is the source of transformation, not rejection, not judgement, not saying you are not good enough, you need to be better.

We don't say to wheat, be better than you are. This is where Monsanto is wrong, because Monsanto says to wheat, you are not good enough. I'll engineer you to make you better. They won't accept wheat as it is. That is why Vandana Shiva and the seed movement are setting out to stop Monsanto because they don't accept nature as nature is, and people as people are. This is why education is a big problem. Universities and schools want you to be educated, because you are not good enough. So you want a PhD. or MA.

Was Jesus Christ a PhD.? Did Jesus Christ have an MA? He was Jesus Christ, he did not need an MA or PhD. Did Buddha go to Harvard? Did Buddha get a PhD? Why do you want to spoil people's minds? Most of the problems of the world today are created by the highly educated people. Who created nuclear weapons? Highly educated people from Harvard, Cambridge and Oxford, and big universities.

Acceptance as the key

So, all these problems are created by not accepting people as they are. Indigenous people have wisdom, they learn from nature, they have compassion, they help each other, they have beautiful crafts, music, singing. All the traditional crafts are without institutionalised schooling and education. If you want to learn about this, read a wonderful book by Ivan Illich called *Deschooling Society*.

Schools and universities are creating this idea of not accepting yourself as you are. We want to get better and better. There is no better or worse, you are what you are, and you participate. When you do gardening, you participate with the soil, when you paint, you participate with colours and imagination.

Universities and schools have become enemies of creativity. They don't allow any imagination, they just want you to learn yesterday's academic knowledge. Libraries are full of stale knowledge. They are ok, they can provide a little information. But real education comes through participation in life. If you want to be a musician, you don't need to go to school to learn singing. If you want to write you don't have to go to school to be a writer, you write. I did not go to a university, and I did not learn speaking at university, I learned to speak by speaking. You learn by doing, not by academic, intellectual knowledge. Learn by doing, learn by experiencing.

Mahatma Gandhi's education model was quite different. He wanted education to be changed. This British education was training people to become employees, to do jobs, whereas the Gandhian idea is not jobs, not employment, but livelihood. Livelihood is participation. Be yourself and participate with others. Building relationships, learning by doing, learning by head, heart and hands, that's a Gandhian.

For a maker, consumption is not a vice

I: Enterprises preach a new religion called consumerism. How can we avoid being destroyed by consumerism? At the same time all activity is somewhere tied to consumption, isn't it?

Satish: When you are not a maker, then you get into the trap of consumerism. What we need to do is to become makers. When you make something, you are participating. If you make food then eating is not consumerism, but if you don't make your food then you are just consuming. So, when people say you are a consumer, you say, "No, I am a maker."

We don't want a consumerist society; we want a society of makers. And when you become a maker then consumption is celebration. When you build a house and sleep in it you create a beautiful house. If you create beautiful food and consume it, it is not consumption, it is a celebration. If a mother prepares food and if we all sit around at the table and appreciate her cooking, that is celebration. We have to replace consumerism with making and celebration.

The word 'poet' means maker. A poet is not the only the person who can put nice words on a page. Poetry is something fresh, something with imagination and creativity, something from your own heart. In the same way, if you make a garden with your own imagination and creativity, with your own heart and skills, your garden becomes poetry.

Your kitchen becomes poetry, your life becomes poetry. The Greek word 'poesis' means to make; 'autopoesis' means self-making. So we are all poets if we make.

At the moment, all the making is given to machines. In the Western world, particularly the modern world, making is a chore, a drudgery. Mahatma Gandhi said making is creativity, not a chore. Making a beautiful table or a pair of shoes is not a chore – these sandals [*pointing to the sandals he was wearing*] are made by hand, in Kolhapur [a district in India's Maharashtra State], and see how lovely they are, a work of art, everything is hand-stitched. Making should be a joy, a pleasure.

Consumerism is not good for the mind, not good for the health.

Also, once machines make, they are so hungry, they go on making. One cloth company burnt 200 tons of clothes. Because they had so much they could not sell it all. What a waste. Machines go on making, making, making, but humans will make only what you need. You can make only a limited amount with your hands. So, replace consumerism with making. Participation, making, then celebration.

Relationship in production

I wear these *chappals** as a celebration – wow, thank you, maker, these are lovely *chappals* that you have made. When I look at them, it is very good on my eyes, and good for my feet. I celebrate, I thank the maker. Traditionally, I would go to the shoemaker and give him the size of my foot, and he would say, ok, I have taken the size, come in five days' time, I'll make it for you. Then I go back, thanking him. There is a relationship in the making. In consumerism there is no relationship.

And without relationship, what is life? Life is all about relationship. There should be a relationship between humans and the materials we use, a relationship between the shirt and the body. It is not just fashion, it's a relationship. So, consumerism has to be replaced by making, by participation, by celebration.

I: How might you inspire others to follow those practices?

Satish: There are a number of things you have to do. Number one, you have to be a radiator. You have to be inspired yourself. If you are not inspired yourself, you can't inspire others. So, the first step is, are you inspired? Be inspired yourself, that is number one. Number two, the way to talk to other people needs skill. And the skill of conversation is that you don't look at the other person as somebody who will agree with you, or as somebody who is in the dark and doesn't know what to do, as if to say "I know, and you don't". With that you create a gap, and they will close the door. They will close their ears, they will not listen to you. So, to have a skilful conversation, do not think they are closed, do not think they are inferior.

Don't think they are in the dark. They are human beings. Whatever they are, they are human beings. You have to create a kind of trust between yourselves. So, generate trust first. To generate trust, say to the person you want to talk to, "Let's go and have a cup of tea together, somewhere." And don't start with ecology and *swadeshi*, and values and peace. Start with, "How are you? How are your parents, how is your wife? How are your children? Where have you been on this holiday?" Start to warm them up. They need to feel that you are a friend. Then you start to talk about Trump, or Brexit or something later. Something light. If you don't have the skill, or if they are closed, if they give resistance, they are not to be converted to peace or anything.

Preaching does not work

So, be yourself, radiating, inspired, and then learn the skills of communication. And see what problems others have. How can you help them? If you are prepared to help somebody, they will become your friend, they will listen to you. But preaching is not the answer. The answer is communication, conversation, dialogue, friendship, helping them and then inspiring them. That is how you inspire.

The third is, you must also learn the skill of communicating through writing. Learn to write. Mahatma Gandhi wrote eighty volumes, a big library. He published *Indian Opinion, Harijan Sevak*, weekly papers. He would write weekly. He would write postcards. Learn the skill of writing ... poetry, essays, your ideas ... in a beautiful, accessible, persuasive, inspiring way. My book, *No Destination,* sold 50,000 copies. Many a time I am told, "I read your book, it was very nice." I learned to write. So, learn to write, poetry, essays, novels, whatever. Arundhati Roy, [the noted Indian author best known for her 1997 book *The God of Small Things*, which won the Man Booker Prize] ... what does she do? She writes, beautifully.

The art of organisation

Next, learn to speak and learn to organise. You organise, the way Vandana Shiva has organised this place [Earth University at Navdanya Farms in Dehradun] or Schumacher College. You organise something where people are invited, can be restful, eat good food, sleep well and then have a good conversation together.

You organise something like Navdanya, or Friends of the Earth, or a movement or ashram or a community, a college. In that way you bring people in. At Schumacher College. 15,000 people have come over the last 26 years. And now they are our representatives and ambassadors all over the world. So, you have to organise something like that, and it is not a one-day commitment; it is a life-long commitment.

You can't say I want to change the world tomorrow. That is not possible. Even the Buddha did not change the world completely, even Jesus Christ did not change the world completely, Mahatma Gandhi did not change the world completely. But he changed it a lot. He inspired many people. Don't think that you can inspire people just like that, it is a life-long commitment. You are starting your journey, start now, learn the skills of communication, conversation, writing, speaking, organising and being. These are the ways to inspire people.

I: How do you keep yourself inspired when we see so much suffering in the world? We see climate change, environmental destruction, a pandemic, then people withdrawing from agreements, like Donald Trump has in the US.

Satish: I keep my inspiration by seeing problems as an opportunity. Thank goodness there is Trump. Now we can speak about something and address the problem. Thank goodness there is climate change and global warming. If this was not there, what would we do? Thank goodness there is Monsanto, we can speak against it. If these people were not there, if there was no suffering, there would be no happiness.

You experience happiness only when there is suffering. I keep myself inspired by seeing negative as an opportunity to light the candle. If there is no darkness, I have no inspiration to light the candle, to put the switch on, to do something. Only because of negative situations do we have the opportunity to do something about them, be an activist. How will you be an activist if there is nothing to be active about? If all were Mother Teresa, Buddha or Gandhi, and there was no Trump, no Monsanto, no negativity and no problem, we would have nothing to do. So our activism, our action, is inspired because there is need for it, because things are not perfect, so we can always make things better and better. That way I keep myself inspired.

I: Do you believe we can inspire big corporations and international institutions to make a change?

Satish: My thinking is that you won't change corporations very easily; it is better to develop alternatives, and when you have developed alternatives and they are interesting and attractive and accessible, then …

Creating alternatives

Take, for example, universities; you can't change universities, but you can create a Schumacher College. You can create Bija Vidyapeeth [Earth University], you can create alternatives, and when there are enough alternatives, the big corporations will not have opportunities. So instead of saying 'no Coca-Cola', create a nice drink in the local area for the local people, which is healthy and delicious. Then people will not buy Coca-Cola. If people don't buy Coca-Cola, then Coca-Cola will collapse. So, creating alternatives is the way to combat corporations and capitalism, instead of banging your head against big corporations with vested interests. They want capitalism, they want money and profit, they will sell anything. So, just criticising is not enough. Criticise, yes. Say why we are creating alternatives, because this is not good. Mahatma Gandhi said, "I am criticising British imperialism and colonialism, but I want to create a new India, which is arts, crafts, agriculture, good education, without a caste* system, without domination of women, without all these things which are a curse on our society." If the British only went away but we did not remove these problems, and Indians were ruling with the same principles, then we would be no better. Gandhi always insisted on creating alternatives, what he called a constructive programme of removing untouchability*, creating arts and crafts and agriculture and bringing women into the main active society. This was his approach, and with your constructive programme you then make a critique of what is wrong in our society and why we are creating constructive programmes and alternatives. That is why I say universities are no good as they are conditioning our people to go and work for capitalism and big business and destroy the world.

We create alternatives like Schumacher College and Bija Vidyapeeth, so we critique and we create at the same time.

I: Does the same approach hold when it comes to change in international organisations/institutions, such as WTO?

Satish: The United Nations can be a good thing, because the UN is different from the WTO. The WTO is controlling. The UN is an international organisation which is enabling and bringing people together in a forum for conversation, discussion and ideas, although there are many problems with the UN. It is dominated by the Security Council, and so on.

But it is a forum for people to come together. The WTO is not a forum; it is a rule, a regulation. You can be taken to court if you don't follow WTO rules. The WTO can even take governments to court. I think international organisations will change too by the creation of alternatives. That is why Vandana Shiva has created this farm, and she is asking many people to save (indigenous) seeds. That is the alternative to Monsanto. Save your seeds; if you just bang on about Monsanto it is not much. Critiquing Monsanto must be accompanied by creating your own seed banks, saving your seeds and promoting biodiversity, cultural diversity, agroecology and so on. If you do not create alternatives then criticism is just one-sided, not enough. Creating alternatives is as essential as critiquing, if not more so.

I: Do not enterprises buy politicians to make laws in favour of them?

Satish: Yes, these people give money to politicians who, when they are in power, favour the big companies. That is why we need *swaraj**, or local self-rule, at every level of government. The central government should be like the thread in the necklace, not seen, but holding everything together. The necklace of each community, of each state, each locality, should shine. They should be as self-reliant as possible with only a little co-ordination required on the national or international scale. But rule should be *swaraj*, self-rule, self-organised, self-managed, local-level – that's the Gandhian idea.

So the role of governments should be that of enabling solidarity, communication, one of coordination and not imposition. It should be a forum, not a ruling. Maximum power at the bottom, minimum power at the top. Government should not bother people. It should just stay there, and if people want to use it, they can use it. So, make maximum freedom for local communities, and minimum interference and minimum rule, on a forum basis. It should be government with a light touch.

I: You have been advocating Gandhian ideals for a long time. Do you think some change will happen? Do you think the world is ready for these ideas? It can be difficult to be in a minority and preserve your ideas, like you do in the UK

Satish: Yes, the first thing is to say that things have improved. When I started editing *Resurgence* and I was writing about solar energy, there was no solar energy in Britain. There was not a single solar panel or a single windmill producing energy. Now 25% of the energy in Britain is renewable energy. A big change. Earlier in England, if I said I am vegetarian, they would say, "What do we feed you? What do you eat? Do you eat chicken? Do you eat fish? What do we feed you?" They had no idea how to feed a vegetarian. Now, after 25 to 30 years, any restaurant in a small town, in the menu, has 'V' for vegetarian. Lots of changes have happened. In Kyoto, in Copenhagen, governments failed to make any agreement about global warming. In Paris in 2016, 198 countries said that global warming is a man-made, human-made problem and we have to address it. Agreement. So, things are changing for the better. There is much more understanding about the environment today, much more organic farming today than there was before.

There is much more interest in good food today than before. So, I think things are changing. Not entirely. The WTO is still there, Coca-Cola and McDonald's are still there. Never mind. We have to keep going. So, with hope, with activism, we can make a change, some transformation in our consciousness, and there are very many good examples. When I was a young man, we were standing in front of the South African embassy in Trafalgar Square, protesting against apartheid. Nobody thought at that time that one day Nelson Mandela could become the president of a new South Africa. Nobody thought at that time, when I met Martin Luther King, 40 years ago, that a black man could be president of the US, and Barack Obama came to the White House.

There are many examples – the Berlin wall came down, the Soviet empire is gone. So, change can happen, does happen, has happened, will happen. We have to be part of the change, part of the solution, rather than be passive and be part of the problem. So, we have to be activists, remain optimists. If you want to be an activist, you have to be an optimist. You cannot be hopeless and say nothing can change, everything is going wrong, everything is bad, what can I do – that is not activism.

An activist has to be an optimist

To be an activist, as I said before, refine your skills to win over people who are not in agreement with you – through friendship, through good writing, through good music. John Lennon said, "Imagine, give peace a chance." He brought a lot of change. Mahatma Gandhi went to jail as a bride goes to the wedding chamber, happy. Martin Luther King, Mother Teresa –

these are our examples – they worked in difficult situations when people were not in agreement with them.

Everybody thought Mahatma Gandhi was a fool. The British Empire, so big, so powerful, the sun never sets on the British Empire, and you think your spinning wheel can change the British Empire, they said. But hundreds and thousands of people started to spin the wheel and burn British-made cloth, made a big bonfire, and India became independent. So, never give up hope. You have power, your power is unlimited. You are a Buddha, you are a Gandhi, you are a Beethoven, a Shakespeare, you are a Neruda, a Vandana Shiva, a Satish Kumar, everyone has capabilities. We don't have to give up. We can stand, we can speak, we have to have the courage of our conviction. If we succeed, thank goodness; if we don't succeed, we tried. Never any problem.

We tried. If you don't try you will regret it. I can say to my children, I tried, I went around the world for peace, and my tea bags are still there. Nuclear weapons have not been used, so I had some influence there. So, always try your best; this is your contribution. It's not the caring that creates the problem. The moment you start caring, the solution begins. When somebody is ill, you think, the person is very ill, what can I do? Just care for the person. If they get better, it is in God's hands. But you are caring, you are washing their feet, washing their body, you are giving them food, changing their clothes, you are caring. So our job is to care for the Earth, for the people, trees, food ... caring, caring, caring.

Sharing, I have talked about. After sharing, also caring. That's all we can do. We are not in charge of the world. Buddha and Jesus Christ and Mahatma Gandhi were not able to solve all the problems of the world, but they did something. So we can do something, that's all we can do.

CHAPTER 8:

Centralised Systems Cannot be the Answer for India

Big cities and big business following in the footsteps of the West cannot solve India's problems, whether they are caste* equalities or health matters, says Satish Kumar. Why should the rural poor become wage slaves in cities, cut off from their land, their soil, their near and dear? The concept of small is beautiful was behind Gandhi's solutions for India, something that holds good even today.

I: What do you say to those who believe that India cannot now afford to follow the alternative, 'small is beautiful' path as it has not achieved all-round development yet? That India cannot resolve its issues of poverty if it does not embark on building massive infrastructure and massive, powerful organisations?

Satish: The 'small is beautiful' idea is only related to organisations. A small organisation, but a big mind. The idea should be big. Gandhi's ideas were very big. But when he talked about village *swaraj, gram swaraj** and village economy, he wanted villages to remain small. The moment you become a big city, like Mumbai, Kolkata, Chennai, Delhi, it becomes a jungle. The air is polluted, the water is polluted, the services, energy consumption, consumerism, all these things become big. So big organisations, big cities, become wasteful and bureaucratic and do not allow human aspirations, imagination and creativity to flourish.

Therefore, keep your organisation small, but have solidarity, have interconnection, have communication. There is no problem with big thinking, big vision, but we need small organisations. If you are teaching in a school, and your school has 2,000 children, the children become numbers. But if the school has 200 children and you have ten schools of 200 children each, that is better than one school of 2,000 children.

In the same way, if you have a huge hospital, the patients become numbers and there is bureaucracy. It is better to have many, many small hospitals. In the villages, small towns and market towns, where there are 10,000 to 50,000 people. But when you have populations like 5 million and 10 million in a city, in Mexico City there are 40 million people living together, it becomes a jungle. There is no human relationship, human connection, warmth, human community. In the big cities you don't even know your neighbour, and you have lived next to each other for forty years and have never known them. So 'big' has a very destructive and unimaginative aspect.

But ideas must be big, the mind and heart must be big, and communication will be big. You can print as many copies of your *Harijan Sevak* or *Indian Opinion* as you want. If *Indian Opinion* becomes very big and bureaucratic, then make it like a newspaper, with multi-city editions, each locally printed, locally organised, locally edited, with some local news in each, so it is not one newspaper for all of India but many local papers run by maybe one big organisation. You can have a decent life system if your economy is decent.

'Small is beautiful' is another way of saying that a system should be decentralised, the economy should be decentralised, politics, education, should be decentralised. If it is centralised, then only a few people at the top will have control and all the other people are servants of the system. So we become slaves.

I: To play the devil's advocate, the entire idea of the Enlightenment project was to liberate the individual from the clutches of the state and religion, and that meant, to some extent creating a face-less society. A face-to-face society can be terribly interfering, and you experience that sometimes in India, particularly in small towns and villages, when somebody wants to know from which caste* you are and who your family is ... they are very interfering.

When you improve and make the system complex, the market is the institution which resolves problems, without any scope for intervention or interventionists, and an individual enjoys the freedom provided by a faceless society. You create systems and arrangements where I don't come in the way of your liberty and you don't come in the way of my liberty.

Satish: I think that the ideal of the Age of Enlightenment has totally failed. That idea of a free individual and faceless society has created isolation, disconnection and exploitation. So, individuals don't know each other. They just come to the factory or office as individuals standing on the conveyor belt, pushing the button. Or they are stuck to Facebook and their smartphone. They are even sending messages to their colleagues in the next room – they are not talking to each other. The age of enlightenment was a reaction against the tyranny of institutionalised religion, and also a reaction against the tyranny of rulers, like the kings, and so on. When something starts as a reaction it often goes wrong, and I think the Age of Enlightenment has gone wrong. It has created a faceless society, and therefore humanity is suffering much more from lack of community, resulting in individualism, depression, isolationism and so on. Science without some constraint and limit, and without purpose and meaning behind it, can lead us to disaster. Science has created technology which has led to nuclear weapons, to genetic engineering and many other destructive and polluting industries.

I: But science has also fought polio, TB and enabled us to provide healthcare of an order that our forefathers could not.

Satish: If science was informed by spiritual, ethical, moral values, it would do all those things without creating nuclear weapons, genetic engineering and so on.

I: Science claims to be objective, value-neutral.

Satish: That is not true. Science is almost a religion. Science has become a dogmatic religion. Scientists are no longer open to truth. They believe in their evolution, they believe in their neo-Darwinian theory; they are as much believers as Hindus are believers in God or Christians believers in Jesus Christ. Take Richard Dawkins [author of the 1976 book *The Selfish Gene*], for example. He believes, with a closed mind. Scientists are quite often closed-minded, and they are servants, in fact slaves, of big industry and the military. Large numbers of scientists are employed by the military, and many scientific and technical inventions from which we benefit, like computers, are the results of military science.

Scientists have become the servants of commerce and the military.

So I would say that the ideal painted of the Age of Enlightenment has not been implemented in practice – it is just an idea. They have not liberated human beings, they have individualised, isolated and disconnected them. I don't think we live in a society of liberated individuals. We live in a society of isolated and disconnected individuals.

I: What is the spiritual part in science that you see?

Satish: I say that science needs spirituality, but spirituality also needs science. Religious people become fundamentalists without a scientific outlook. That is why we have Christian fundamentalism, Hindu fundamentalism, Muslim fundamentalism, Buddhist fundamentalism. Everywhere you see this fundamentalism. Very narrow minded, very dogmatic, and very sectarian – "My truth the only truth, what I believe is the truth". But it may not be the truth, it's just your belief. So, if you have a scientific outlook, mixed with spirituality and wisdom and understanding, then science and wisdom and spirituality can go together, dance together, work together, and that would be my ideal.

I: If we recall the 1945 debate* just before India became independent between Mahatma Gandhi and the man who would become India's first Prime Minister, Jawaharlal Nehru. Gandhi says reject Western civilisation while Nehru tells Gandhi, sorry, but this is outdated. I have a different country to handle, different circumstances to handle. What is the guarantee that without a decided interventionist approach, the 'ignorant', 'unhealthy', 'insanitary', 'superstitious' set of villages would have come out and become 'enlightened'?

Satish: All these terms you use – superstitious, unenlightened – all these are ideas imposed by the scientific Age of Enlightenment. I lived in a village, grew up in a village, my mother was an illiterate woman. I don't think village society is superstitious all the time, or unenlightened, or bigoted. This view is a kind of imposition by 'educated, civilised' human beings, and that civilisation is no longer really civilised, but it is supposed to be.

Just as the Age of Enlightenment has not proved to be ideal, village society too needs a lot of reform. That reform has to be in the areas of caste* discrimination, religious discrimination, exploitation of the poor by the rich, and landlordism. You can bring about reform without throwing out the baby with the bathwater, without throwing away your spirituality, your ethics, your moral principles, your unity of life and your solidarity. Without throwing these values out in the name of enlightenment and progress and development, you can bring reform. That has been done in the past, when Buddha and Mahavira encouraged a large number of people to move away from the Hindu idea of animal sacrifice and become vegetarian.

This was reform within the traditional structure. I am not saying that village society or society before the Age of Enlightenment was wonderful and perfect. Not by any means. But what has been put in its place is like going from the frying pan into the fire, and that is not the answer. What we need is the third alternative. The third alternative is where you are liberated in spirit. I am free. The moment I realise that I am free, I am free. In modern society – faceless, atheist society – people are not free. People are slaves of their wages, they are salary slaves, and they are bound.

The modern-day wage slave

People go to work, but they don't like to work; they do work which they don't like, but they have to do it, to pay the bills. We have become wage slaves. So, in this so-called Age of Enlightenment, we are not enlightened at all. It is a kind of dark age. I would say we need a third alternative. We are not going back to the caste-ridden, superstitious society which you talked about, because that is not ideal. But at the same time, a faceless, isolated, disconnected, materialistic, consumer society is not the answer either. We have to have something that is a bit saner and much more intelligent.

CHAPTER 9:

Caste-politics, Justice, Health and Technology

Mahatma Gandhi and B.R. Ambedkar* did not always agree on caste*. Certainly Gandhi was against caste-based discrimination and was appalled at the way lower-caste people were treated, but he did not repudiate caste, as he felt each community in India had evolved to have a distinctive vocation and way of life, which needed be held in the same regard as those of other castes.

Ambedkar was a Dalit*, a community previously considered 'untouchable'. He rose to be head of the collegium that drafted the Indian Constitution. He fought to bring Dalits out of their plight, encouraging their mass conversion to Buddhism, giving rise to the great Dalit-Buddhist movement in India. He also encouraged their migration to urban centres to escape their wretched treatment in the villages.

Satish Kumar here appreciates the Gandhian approach.

I: Ambedkar told Gandhi that his theory of love was not going to work and advised the Dalits to simply leave their villages and move to the urban areas. What is your view on this?

Satish: I think Ambedkar was wrong. If you exchange one slavery for another kind, that's not the answer. What he advocated is that you become the slave of the factory system, the machine system, the urbanised system, where you become a wage slave. What I am saying is that the Harijans*, the Dalits and the scheduled* castes have the right to live in the village, have a right to have land on which they can work and on which their house can stand. And if they don't have land, then houses must be built, their jobs protected and respected. There should be dignity in making shoes. I was saying this morning, those *chappals** are beautifully made. Why is it that if you use a computer you are very highly respected, if you work in a bank, you are highly respected, but if you are making pots or shoes or building a house or growing food or you are a farm labourer, you have no dignity? That must change. Ambedkar was wrong to say Dalits must go to the city, or that Dalits must have a separate state. Jinnah, founder of Pakistan, said Muslims should have a separate state. That was also wrong, in my view.

I: But facelessness in the city, from Ambedkar's point of view, would have been better than to be humiliated by a neighbour in the village. Ambedkar may have argued that facelessness is an equaliser for everybody and, whatever their caste, all are slaves of the same machine.

Satish: But there is a better alternative.

I: Not from the position he was in and the way he saw it at that time.

Satish: But he did not work to create a better alternative. At that time, cities were not as awful as they are today, but cities cannot be the answer. If you bring so many people to the cities, they have to depend on fossil fuels and all the energy systems, and food is not produced there. Somebody has to make shoes, somebody has to make pots. Who is going to make them? So, bringing dignity and paying them better wages is a better solution. Why should a banker be paid higher than a farmer? Why should a bureaucrat in a government office be paid higher? This is what Gandhi said in *Hind Swaraj**. They should have equal value...

I: Yes, Ruskin's second point. A lawyer and a barber must get the same wages. ["That a lawyer's work has the same value as the barber's, inasmuch as all have the same right of earning their livelihood from their work."]

Satish: A lawyer does not eat more. Why should the lawyer be paid more? A lawyer does not wear ten jumpers and twenty shoes and have five motor cars at the same time. He uses one motor car or one pair of shoes. So, why should a lawyer or banker be paid more?

I: On this Dalit point, to again be the devil's advocate – please don't take offence – you are saying this because you are not from the Dalit caste. What kind of waiting period do we have, to get justice, to better our lives?

Satish: No waiting period. We want change now. Can you send your Dalits? How many million people are in the cities? Who will provide houses for them? It is a pipe dream. Ambedkar had a pipe dream. How many Dalits were there at that time? How many million? Ten million, 20 million? Where are you going to build 20 million houses immediately, because Ambedkar says so? He is not a dictator.

I: No, he was not a dictator. What he was saying was to slowly migrate.

Satish: Slowly migrate ... but why not slowly change the system and bring dignity to the people? This is what Vinoba said. Vinoba said that we should give land and homes to the landless, and wells to the landless ... *daan* and *bhoodan**. We should create a system by which people can remain authentic and integrated with nature and land.

I: There is an issue of mindset in this, even today. We have first-hand accounts of emancipated Dalits, who are protected by the Indian Constitution and have been given reservations. A few joined the IAS [*Indian Administrative Service – the post-Independence version of the Indian Civil Service, considered the crème de la crème of the Indian bureaucracy*], and other services like the Indian Police Service, but they are not offered a plot of land in high-caste neighbourhoods in their villages even if they are willing to pay. How does one respond to this?

Satish: The thing is, whether it is Dr Ambedkar or anybody else, or the black people, there has been slavery of a 100 years or 500 years. We have a problem, a problem which has been brewing or simmering for 500 years, and you want the solution in five minutes. That is impatience.

I: It is everybody's right not to suffer for even one minute longer, if they can help it.

Satish: For this, you have to sacrifice yourself. Gandhi lived like a Dalit. He was not a Dalit but he lived in a hut, like a Dalit lives. Vinoba lived like a Dalit, wearing a loincloth – a very simple life. So, we who are advocating equality and dignity need to identify ourselves with the poor and the low-caste and the Dalits and live simple lives ourselves rather than try to bring them to another level and say, "You must live like a rich man. You must live in Bombay or Delhi or Kolkata, and have Ambani's house." It's not going to happen. It is a pipe dream. So why not give people dignity, land, and pay them fair wages? Why should shoes, food and pots be cheap, and computers and cars expensive? Why do we not value the work which ordinary people are producing, which are essential for our lives? We cannot live without food and shoes; we can live without computers. But we pay a high value for these mechanised products.

I: Ambedkar's was not an economic argument at all, because even if you provide for Dalits economically, the way people treat them has not changed...

Satish: Give them a fair wage. Give them social justice.

I: Social justice is not coming. Economic justice can be driven.

Satish: Economic justice and social justice go together. Dignity of labour, and dignity and respect ... for all people are humans before they are Harijan, Dalit, Scheduled* Caste, Brahmin or merchant. We must respect every human equally. And that is what I would say to Ambedkar. They are humans, you must respect them. It will take time. It is a situation, a reality, something which has brewed over 500 years or 1,000 years, you cannot solve it overnight. Whatever your solution, even what Ambedkar suggests, that solution will not happen overnight. So, why not try to find a better alternative which brings economy and dignity and all those things to people where they are rather than uprooting them and placing them in an alien place where they have no family, no connection, no land, no nature. That is not the solution.

I: You would agree that discrimination of this nature, the caste-based kind that we see, is violence?

Satish: Discrimination is violence. Absolute violence. It is institutionalised violence. Caste discrimination, race discrimination, discrimination under any name, is institutionalised violence. It is a much worse kind of violence than hitting somebody, the worst kind of violence. Human life has to have dignity, there is no other question. And bring that dignity and do not look for a short cut. Even in the cities, there are millions of people living in the slums. Is it any good for them? Are they better? Are you going to create for everybody in Bombay, beautiful houses for all Dalits? It is a pipe dream. It is wrong. Neither is it practical, nor ideal.

I: To move to a scientific issue. How am I to respond to the suggestion that it is only from the fission reactor and the fission bomb that we someday get fusion energy that is very clean. This is at the root of what

science takes to evolve to a cleaner future. It is only from fossil fuel emissions that we will go to the electric car.

Satish: I call it the techno-fix, technological fix. You cannot fix human problems with technology. If your greed, your attachments and your desire for more and more continue, and however much you have, you are still discontented and you want even more, whatever energy you use, whether it is solar, renewable, fission or fusion, will not be a solution.

The solution is human. It is in your heart. How much do you want? How much progress do you want? How much development do you want? How many houses do you want? Ambani has a twenty-seven-storey house, is that not enough for you? You want more. He is not satisfied, not contented. There are 1.3 billion people in India. If we have 1 billion people all living like Ambani, still we will be worse off. So where do you want to go? The solution is a middle way. We want everybody to have good food, good clothes, well-made shoes, beautiful houses, good education, good access to medicine ... elegant simplicity, I call it. Everyone must have the basics, and beyond that go for non-material progress, progress in arts, crafts, culture, music, dance, philosophy, literature, poetry ... there is no limit. You can do that.

On different types of energy, we don't know what the problems with fission and fusion will be, we don't know yet. When we mined fossil fuels, we did not know that it would cause global warming and climate change. There is this idea of techno-fixing that thinks all solutions are technological. Solutions are not technological – technology is only an aid to human development. Technology can aid (humans), but human fulfilment will come from my own realisation that I have enough, I am contented, now I must do something better than just have more cars and more goods.

**I: I'll describe a practical issue on the pressure to build more infrastructure in India. In parts of India, more than 45% of Indian women even today give birth without expert care and at home. [*Latest data from the National Family Health Survey (NFHS) shows that the percentage of institutional births has increased in recent years but is still low in many areas. For example, Kishanganj district in Bihar reported only 55% of births in the last five years were in an institution. The NFHS is one of the world's largest surveys and is a collaborative project of the International Institute for Population Sciences, Mumbai, India; ICF, Calverton, Maryland, USA and the East-West Center, Honolulu,*

Hawaii, USA.] That is directly linked to the maternal mortality rate and infant survival rate. If I have to build hospitals for them, I have to build infrastructure. If I have to build infrastructure, I must get a road to go to that infrastructure.

Satish: My solution to that would be to train more midwives and more doctors who can go to people's homes and help to deliver babies safely, rather than create more hospitals and bring our women to hospitals to deliver. My daughter was delivered at home, and my son was delivered in hospital, and I found that delivery at home was much better. For my daughter's birth, a midwife came and a doctor came. If they can come to the house, the doctor and midwife will be in the service of the mother, not the mother in the service of and dependent on the convenience of the doctor and nurse. Sometimes babies are delivered by Caesarean section, and the birth has to be in working hours so the doctor can deliver them. That is going too far. I would say natural birth, at home, safe birth, with the assistance of the doctor and midwife present. Millions of people have delivered at home in the past, hospitals are only 100 or 200 years old.

I: But at a higher rate of mortality...

Satish: But the quality of life we now live is not good. Modern civilisation, modern culture ... what it is trying to do is replace one problem with another problem. What I am saying is don't replace one problem with another; find a proper, dignified, honest, authentic, true solution. And the true solution, for reduced mortality rate and so on, is to bring the assistance to the mother where she is. The mother is more important than the hospital or doctor.

I: The doctor will need roads to go to the village, vehicles to go there.

Satish: You can have trained nurses and doctors in every village. You can bring the training of nursing there. It need not be Western style. You can have the traditional style too. There are ways. Wisdom needs to be used.

I: We still are doing it. My [Dr. Sudarshan Iyengar's] wife is a midwife trainer.

Satish: We need to do more training; more midwives should have village training. They do not have to go to the city for training.

I: We are also training them in identifying risks, so that they can transport the woman if they see risks that they cannot handle, where there is necessity for medical intervention.

Satish: I am not an extremist. I am trying to find a middle way, and the middle way is not to go all the way to technological solutions and technological fix.

I: Not blindly ... It is not a panacea.

Satish: That is what is happening now. Use technology well. We need science and technology. Use them with wisdom. We were in Ghanerao [*Ghanerao Rawla castle in the small village of Ghanerao in Rajasthan is a magnificent showcase of Rajpur architecture in marble and red sandstone built in 1606*] which is a small royal palace. They built it over 50 or 60 years. They had patience, they had imagination and creativity, and they had skills. Humans made it by hand, without any (modern) technology. Nowadays, you go to Delhi or Mumbai, and you see new houses ... there is no imagination, no skills, no craftsmanship. They have a lot of technology but no imagination. I am not against science and technology. But science and technology without wisdom and without imagination will not bring a solution. America had a lot of technology but no wisdom.

I: Where would you place Baba Ramdev? [*Baba Ramdev is a yoga instructor who has sought to popularise ayurveda and later launched a range of products under the brand Patanajali, giving leading FMCG brands some tough competition in the Indian market.*]

Satish: I have not met him, so I don't know him enough. I have heard that he has a television programme and he has Patanjali products.

I: He is a Rs 10,000 crore (USD 1.3 billion) business now and has said that he is going to have grow tenfold in the next ten years.

Satish: And they are all controlled from one place?

I: He is the master!

Satish: Centralised?

I: He is the production boss. Many Indians take pride in how he is poised to give Unilever a run for its money.

Satish: I don't know enough. I can't really comment. Vandana Shiva met him. There may be some good things in there. But I believe in small is beautiful, I believe in a small-scale decentralised system. If it is centralised and on a large scale, then it is replacing Unilever with Ramdev or Patanjali. That is not the answer. If Patanjali and Ramdev can set a different kind of example, and have many small, autonomous, self-organised units, running their own imaginative, creative projects inspired by Ramdev, that would be fine. But if you have centralised control, then I don't think it is right. I am a decentralist, a small-is-beautiful-principle person.

I: Do you see the Ambanis and the Tatas [two of India's largest and oldest business houses] as similar? In the Indian context most people are of the view they have different ways of doing business, as far as their ethos goes. The Tatas are supposed to run on a trust principle, a lot of the profits go back to the Tata Trusts, which are in the service of the people; Ambani is all for multi-storey buildings.

Satish: Tatas are giving money to trusts … but the family still controls?

I: A majority of the shareholding is with the trusts.

Satish: But still, they are in big business, steel, cars, Jaguar Land Rover, etc. This business model might have a different ethos, but the impact of that business on the environment or on the people is not that much different. They are doing philanthropy, which is good, slightly better than Ambanis, but I would say that their business model is not ecological or socially just.

I: Have you ever had conversations with Ratan Tata or with JRD before him? Or with the Ambanis, with any of the Birlas?

Satish: No. Never with any of them. I used to know Shanti Prasad Jain quite well. He was chairman of the *Times of India* … I used to know Ramkrishna Dalmia [*one of the wealthiest businessmen at the time of Indian independence in 1947, having built businesses in sugar, cement and other areas*]. I talked to these people as a Gandhian and working with Vinoba. I said to them that their motivation and intention needs to be not just making profit but sustaining jobs, work. I have talked to them about all those things but without much success.

I: It is amazing that you say this about Shanti Prasad Jain. His group, it is said, is at the forefront of turning the news media into a money-making machine.

Satish: And they are Jains, can you imagine!

I: Do you feel like sometimes preaching to them? Engaging with them?

Satish: Preaching will not help. I have met some other people. I met Mrs. Rajashree Birla [*mother of Kumar Mangalam Birla, who heads one of India's largest business conglomerates, the Aditya Birla group, and leader of the Aditya Birla Centre for Community Initiatives and Rural Development, the group's apex body responsible for development projects*] not long ago, through a common friend. My way of communicating is to make a personal friendly relationship first. Preaching makes people defensive. But if you become more friendly, have a conversation and dialogue, without preaching, then they open their hearts and listen to you. So, I engage first on a human level and only then on an intellectual level.

I: Are you spending a lot of time on this, or do you think it's not an issue?

Satish: I want them to invite me to speak to them. I do sometimes get invitations in England, from the London School of Economics, or the business community invite me to speak and I speak to them. I have spoken at HSBC, Cathay Pacific Airways ... and at some other companies.

I: Would you agree that the absence of many such invitations from India could be reflective of the lack of your engagement with India? After all, you have been away for a long time.

Satish: There are many other wonderful speakers, teachers and communicators in India in the Gandhian movement, in the ecological movement, in the social justice movement. There is no shortage of great, wonderful activists in India. And if the business people are not listening to them, then my influence is very small.

I: But many of these activists are not really satyagrahis [*practitioners of satyagraha, which is non-violent resistance to drive a desired change and seek a new harmony*] **of the kind that Gandhi wished to see, in practice and preaching both. Do you see this as a serious problem?**

Satish: Yes, it is a serious problem. At the moment, we – myself included – don't have a clear strategy. In order to build a movement, you need to have a focus. Martin Luther King's focus was racial discrimination. Nelson Mandela's was apartheid. Gandhi's focus was independence for India. Vinoba's focus was land distribution. The feminist movement was for women's liberation. All these movements had a clear focus. When there is a clear focus then all the other philosophies, values and analyses can be brought to support it. If Gandhi did not have Indian independence clearly in focus, then all these constructive programmes, *Nayi talim** [literally 'new education', a Gandhian initiative to bring basic education to everyone] and others, would not have had the same power. It was because of that focus that many people could follow him, and his constructive programmes gained some reputation.

I: What is the possible focus now?

Satish: Vandana and I are focused on issues concerning globalisation, and we think it is the local economy we have to promote. Globalisation should be the focus, but not everyone at the moment is coming around to it. But that focus has to emerge, you cannot impose it.

I: Maybe you should not say globalisation. Suppose you talk about localisation, *swadeshi*. Do you think that has scope now?

Satish: Yes, that might be another ... ecology movement, climate change has a focus. And in the world, the ecology movement is quite strong.

I: To come to another point, I am told that India is the largest exporter of beef. Did you know that?

Satish: I didn't know that. So, what is [Prime Minister Narendra] Modi doing about it?

I: Today we have a situation where slaughtering cattle is considered such a sacrilege that people suspected of doing it, if they are Muslim, have been lynched. So, stopping violence of one kind has led to violence of another kind. If a poor farmer finds his cow low yielding and not economically viable, he is only going to let it stray free on the roads. So now there is a large number of cows roaming all over our roads, eating plastic out of garbage bins.

Satish: So, first of all, we have to ban plastic. Second, we need to create *gaushalas* [shelters for cows] where these cows can live, and in those *gaushalas*, whatever amount of milk they can give, take it, otherwise feed the calves, and breed new cows which are a bit better yielding, and so on.

I: If you look at their number, it is huge and will double in three years.

Satish: But slaughter is not the answer. It is like saying the population of humans has doubled, so humans should be slaughtered. We don't have land, we don't have jobs, we don't have houses, so do we kill people? You can't. In the same way, in the forest we have too many deer or too many tigers or elephants so we kill them. Killing is not the answer.

I: There is a natural process of limitation.

Satish: But killing cows is not a natural process.

I: What is the greatest ethical problem facing mankind today?

Satish: Violence. Violence towards nature, violence in the name of religion, politics, democracy, capitalism. All these 'isms' are at the moment not adhering to the principle of non-violence, towards yourself, towards other people, towards nature. The caste system and other things you have mentioned are violent towards other people, exploiting other people. The biggest challenge in our society is that we have not accepted the principle of non-violence. We use violence and we produce technology, science, consumer goods, systems, governments, political systems, with violence.

I: Since violence has stayed with us for so long in history, would we be able to argue that violence is a part of human nature?

Satish: Not as an ideal.

I: But it is part of human nature.

Satish: It is, but not as an ideal.

I: It is not the state to be in?

Satish: We always presume our ideal is non-violence, minimising violence. Science and technology and governments and religions are not pursuing that ideal.

CHAPTER 10:

Sarvodaya

Satish Kumar says the concept of Sarvodaya*, a word more or less created (and its concept advocated strongly) by Gandhi, distils the essence of living in harmony with all existence. This has been Satish Kumar's guiding star in most of his ventures. The uniqueness of the concept lies in its not being human-centric, and for this reason alone the word should enter every dictionary of every language in the world.

I: Do you have an interpretation of *Sarvodaya?*

Satish: *Sarva* is a very important word in Gandhian language. It means 'all', like Om. No-one excluded. Everyone included. *Udaya* means wellbeing, upliftment, rising. When the sun rises in the morning, we call it *Suryodaya*. Everybody is uplifted, rising, feeling well. Gandhi's philosophy is called *Sarvodaya*. It is one word. And all the other things like *swaraj**, *swadeshi*, *satyagraha*, then ideas about the soil, soul, society, are all variations of the basic philosophy of *Sarvodaya*. Actually, Mahatma Gandhi created this word. It was originally used in the Jain tradition a long time ago. The Jain tradition, one of whose teachers I said influenced Gandhi, says, '*Sarvodayam tirthamidham smarami*'; *tirth* means pilgrimage, spiritual crossing. So, Jains also have the same thing – all living beings are included, nobody is excluded. *Sarvodaya* is not an anthropocentric philosophy. I repeat: *Sarvodaya is not an anthropocentric philosophy*. Meaning, *Sarvodaya* is not human centred. *Sarvodaya* is not only for humans. *Sarvodaya* is for humans, and for other-than-humans – that is the important part. Whereas all other philosophies, political systems ... are mostly anthropocentric.

Make all isms 'wasms'

The capitalist system is all about capital for humans. Socialism is also about society, human society. Marxism also the same, industrialism and materialism, the same. All isms. But Gandhi said, put no 'ism' with *Sarvodaya*. Make all isms 'wasms'. Gandhi said, I don't want to leave any 'ism' behind me. So, the word *Sarvodaya* has no 'ism'. The moment you make something an 'ism', it becomes static, fixed, unchanging, stagnant. So that is why I say, make all 'isms' into 'wasms'. Buddhism and Hinduism are also 'isms'. The moment you become an 'ism', or an 'ist', like socialist, communist, capitalist, that is no good.

So, Gandhi was advocating the free spirit. I am not carrying on the work of Gandhi, I am carrying on my own work. I am inspired by Gandhi and I learn from Gandhi but what I speak to you is how I understand and appreciate not only Gandhi, but life. So, none of you needs to follow Gandhi. Gandhi did not want any followers. Follow yourself, you have your inner Gandhi, your inner guru. Don't follow any guru, follow your own inner guru.

But learn from all gurus. My wife goes to Thich Nhat Hanh, and brings me lovely books and calligraphy. We get a Tibetan monk coming into our house to teach us, we have a Christian priest who teaches us. We learn from everybody, but we are not followers of anybody. *Sarva* means holistic, everything, whole, all, included. This is a very important point which I want you to remember. So, I have teased out *Sarvodaya* into three words, that is, soil, soul and society.

Three aspects. I put soil at the top, because we are humans, and human means soil. The Latin word for soil is humus. Everybody knows that. And from humus comes human. And so human beings are literally soil beings, they are earthlings. Our body is made of soil. There is no difference between this body and the body of a tree. The tree is soil transformed.

Earth is not a dead rock

The delicious bananas that you are eating are nothing but soil. Soil is the basic element. And all the other elements help of course, water, air, we all need that. But soil is the fundamental. In the modern world, the old-fashioned scientists think differently. There are new-fashioned scientists too, like James Lovelock and Fritjof Capra and Rupert Sheldrake, who don't see soil as dead, but as a living organism. They see Earth as a living organism, as Gaia, a Goddess.

Earth is a Goddess, not just a dead rock. But the old-fashioned scientists say that Earth is a dead rock. And this is why they think soil has no life, and therefore they have to put chemicals and fertilisers and pesticides and all kinds of poisons to make soil fertile. But we don't need anything here. In modern times we have forgotten the importance of soil. Soil is being eroded, on the one hand, left, right and centre, and soil is being poisoned, left, right and centre, on the other hand. This is why we need Vandana Shiva, we need Bija Vidyapeeth [Earth University].

Dirt is not dirty

We need to save seeds, we need to go to organic farms, to Gujarat Vidyapith, where people are learning to touch the soil. If you live in Mumbai, Paris, Frankfurt, London, New York, there is no soil, there is concrete. The soil is dirty, your hands are dirty, you wash them with soap. Your hands are not dirty. Dirt is not dirty, soap is dirty (laughter). You make your hands dirty with the soap. Soil is clean. I put my hands in the soil, I clean my plates with it. My mother always cleaned plates, not with soap, but with soil. When you wash the plates after that, they are clean. Soil is living and we need to revere it, so I put soil as a part of Sarvodaya. Caring for the soil comes before caring for humans, because humans are soil.

Adam also means earth, apart from man. But man comes later, earth comes first. If you go to the universities, Oxford, Cambridge in England, Harvard and Yale in America, University of Paris, University of Moscow, JNU in New Delhi, no mainstream university will consider soil science as a mainstream subject. Most of our education is about business, business management, technology, science, politics, economics. Agriculture is at the bottom. The old-fashioned way of teaching agriculture is to chemicalise and fertilise and use pesticides and tractors and combine harvesters and factory farms. This is not agriculture, it is agri-business.

Most agriculture today is agri-business

I was invited to speak at the Beijing University of Agriculture. At the People's University, there is a department of agriculture. The first question I asked them: 'Are you learning about agriculture, or are you learning about agri-business?' Agriculture has been turned into agri-business. That is not culture. Culture also means soil. If you go to old English dictionaries, you will see culture, cultivating soil, and then as you cultivate soil, that's culture, you cultivate your soul, your imagination, and therefore dance, music, poetry, painting, architecture, all that comes from cultivating your soul. That is culture. But in business, you grow food to sell as a commodity.

So if we want sustainability, happiness, joy, good life, we have to look after the soil. You nourish the soil, preserve and enrich soil. How do you nurture soil – you make compost. Every bit of our kitchen waste and organic waste should go into the compost bin and everything will turn into soil, and that soil fertilises dry soil. So, making compost should be everybody's duty.

It is a duty, a responsibility, to return to the soil what we have taken. So, if you are not putting your kitchen waste and your organic waste back into the soil, you are not replenishing the soil, and our responsibility is to replenish, to nourish soil, not to deplete it. Nature has its own system. All the leaves fall in the autumn and in the winter time they all degrade, biodegrade and become soil. Nature's economy is cyclical. In the autumn you have fruit to eat. What you defecate also goes into the soil. We go to the WC and flush, that is not Gandhian. Mahatma Gandhi designed a toilet which empties into the soil, a compost toilet. Similarly, anything in nature goes back into the soil, everything that we have should go back to the soil.

If anything we are using is not biodegradable, that is a sin against the soil. If you say you do not want to sin, then don't use anything that cannot be reabsorbed and recycled into our soil. So, everything we use should be organic so it can be put back into the soil.

'Soil is my Goddess'

A lot of things here at Bija Vidyapeeth are organic, but the chairs you are sitting on are not organic. I don't think that at Bija Vidyapeeth chairs of this kind should be brought in. Somebody brought them, I forgive them (laughter) but they are not Gandhian. There should be hand-made chairs with wood and straw, like these (points to cane chairs). These carpets can go back into the soil. We call our compost bin a compost palace. The compost palace is built by our son, Mukti. He is a great carpenter, our son. I am delighted to be the father of my son, who has built us a beautiful compost palace. We put all our kitchen waste, all our grass, leaves, etc., and all the waste from our harvest into it. And the compost, within two or three months, becomes beautiful soil, which we put into the garden. That is recycling. That is the soil, and we have to make a new religion of soil. Soil is our religion. Religion is not in the books, Bible, Quran, Bhagavad Gita. Religion is not in the temples. Religion is in the soil. My religion is nature, my religion is soil. I am a devotee of the soil; soil is my goddess.

And, like we ignore soil, we also ignore soul. Tell me about one university where they teach how to nourish the soul. What is your soul? How do you care for your soul? Of course, you can read Thomas Moore's book *Care of the Soul*. Great psychologists like David Hume, James Hillman and Thomas Moore talk about 'care of the soul'. But in our modern industrial, capitalist, communist, socialist, materialist society, none of the universities, nobody, will talk about soul. And if you talk about it, 'wishy washy flaky', they will say, 'You are not real, you are just abstract.' I say no, without soul, without nourishing the soul, without replenishing the soul, our imagination, creativity, art, culture will not flourish.

This is why the modern world, the industrial world, the mechanised, reductionist world of science and technology, of business, of banks, commerce, politics, economics, have all become the enemies of the imagination. There is no place for imagination in factories, banks, big conveyor belts, where you just stand and become a worker, a bureaucrat. In big companies, corporations, multinationals, globalised corporations, human beings have no opportunity, no chance, to use their imagination and creativity. They have to follow the rules. So, I say, care for the soul. Look after yourself, love yourself. Loving yourself is not selfish.

Does anyone have time for anything beautiful?

But where is the time for the soul? Where is the time for yoga? Who has the time for meditation? Who has the time for reading something beautiful? Who has time for singing, for wandering in nature? That's the way you replenish the soul. So, take care of yourself, you are very special. Every one of you is a special gift to this Earth. Don't ignore yourself, don't put yourself down, and don't say. 'I am no good, I am only one small person, what can I do?' No, you are a Buddha, you are a Gandhi, you are a Vandana Shiva, Wangari Maathai, Mother Teresa.

You are very special. Our great teacher in India was Ananda Coomaraswami* [*1877-1947, a historian and a philosopher who introduced Indian art to the West*]. He said, "An artist is not a special kind of person, but every person is a special kind of artist." When you are strong, resilient, happy, joyful, then go out and help the poor, the needy, the sick the hungry. Help the forest, plant the forest, do activism, go to jail, like Martin Luther King, and Mahatma Gandhi and Nelson Mandela went to jail. If you are strong inside, you can do all that.

In order to change the world, you have to be strong. So, before society, I put the soul, you the person. Planet first, the soil is the planet, and then you the person. The ultimate is soil, the planet, and the intimate is the soul. So, I come from the ultimate to the intimate.

Then comes society, which is divided. The world is divided. We are in conflict. In the name of religion, we are divided. As nations, we are divided. We are now dividing ourselves with Brexit. In the name of trade, we are divided. Trump says, America first. What is America? America is made up of 200 nations or 150 nations. People have come from all over the world. America first, then India first, Bhutan first. How can you have 198 nations first? Somebody has to be second and third, and therefore nobody is first and nobody is second and third. We are all equal, one society, one humanity.

We are one humanity that is one society. But we have Christians and Muslims and Jews fighting in Palestine, Shias and Sunnis fighting in Saudi Arabia and there are fights in Yemen, Iran, Syria and Afghanistan. Catholics and Protestants fight. Even among Protestants there is religious fighting. You are supposed to be educated, advanced, PhDs and all that. But what are you doing – dividing! I want society to be one humanity. And see divisions not as divisions but as diversity. Diversity is not to be fought about but to be celebrated. We celebrate being Christians and Hindus and Muslims, we celebrate being American, Russian or Chinese. If the seven billion people on this planet spoke only English, and not hundreds of other languages like Tamil, Bengali, Chinese and Mandarin and so on, it would be boring, everybody speaking one language.

Uniformity is monotony

Everybody doing the same thing ... that would be boring. That is monoculture. Do you want monoculture? If a field has only roses and no wheat, no rice, no vegetables, no bananas, no oranges, only roses – can you survive? We need biodiversity, we need religious diversity, cultural diversity, national diversity, truth diversity. There are millions of truths, everybody has their own truth, why do we say my truth is better than your truth?

So, I put society there, at the end. *Sarvodaya* is described in three words in my book *Soil, Soul, Society: Trinity for Our Time*. Any great movement encapsulates its essence in three words: the French revolution had 'Liberty, Equality, Fraternity', to describe its essence. The American trinity is 'Life,

Liberty and Pursuit of Happiness'. Then you have the trinity of mind, body, spirit. There are many other trinities. So, I thought, what is the trinity which combines totality, the holistic thinking?

A new trinity for our times

Liberty, Equality, Fraternity is not quite holistic, it doesn't have connection with the Earth, the planet and nature. Neither does Mind, Body, Spirit. *My* mind, *my* body, *my* spirit. So I wanted a new trinity for our times, which represents the *Sarvodaya* philosophy of wellbeing for all, the bio-centric, land-centric or nature-centric world view rather than anthropocentric world view.

A Sand County Almanac is a book that talks about these sorts of things. It goes beyond the anthropocentric world view. The universe is not a collection of objects, it is a communion of subjects. We are all in communion, and when we are in communion, we can minimise our violence, anger, pride, ego and fear, and maximise our unity in diversity and we can maximise our love, compassion, generosity, towards each other and towards nature. That is spirituality, ecology, social justice, all coming together. This is the idea of Gandhi, the genius of Gandhi. Gandhi's collected works go into eighty volumes. It's a big body of work, he was a great writer, great thinker and great activist at the same time.

In one word, *Sarvodaya,* he has described all these ideas and much more. It is not Gandhi's idea. As I said, it has come from the ancient language. Gandhi got this idea by reading a wonderful writer in England, called John Ruskin, and his essay *Unto this Last.*

Gandhi read this on a train and was so inspired that he translated it into Gujarati, calling the book *Sarvodaya.* Then it became a beautiful word, it came into Hindi. The word *Sarvodaya* is Sanskrit, so it can be used in any Indian language and all will understand it. I want this *Sarvodaya* included in the English dictionary, the French dictionary, the Russian dictionary, in every dictionary in the world.

In our 'Gandhi and Globalisation' course, we present the new trinity for our times – soil, soul, society.

Three visions

All crises which occur today are a result of separation and disconnection. So first I would like to see, in our schools and universities, a new curriculum, a new syllabus, which sees unity in diversity, and diversity to be celebrated and not turned into division. This is why we started Gujarat Vidyapith and Schumacher College, because modern education is all about separation, disconnection and individualism. We say, we are one human community, one Earth community and we are all members of this Earth, members of one human society and then members of one country, and then members of one family. All that is good. But there is no need to see them in opposition. Make no enemy in the name of religion or nationality. Give no offence because you are American or Russian or North Korean or whatever. All our political problems come from this idea of separation and division. Non-duality and non-division should start. My vision is to change education.

The second area for change will be the media. I think our media is also very responsible (for the state of affairs today). They use such divisive language, particularly the tabloids in England. The press is very nationalistic and very jingoistic, and it always creates separation.

So the second vision for me would be to create an alternative media where we see connections, rather than disconnection and separation. If we can bring that into our understanding then we can embrace whatever your philosophy is, like a part of the big picture. Like in nature, we can embrace roses and thorns, we can embrace matter, we can embrace snakes. We can embrace anything in nature. We cannot say, 'No, no, snake, you can't stay there, or thorns you can't stay there, we only want flowers.' Even something a little difficult ... we can live with it. We don't have to condemn anything. We should try to find harmony and live together.

The third will be an intercultural, inter-faith dialogue. I would like to see a better dialogue between Buddhist, Christian, Jewish, Muslim, all the faiths. They are always putting down other religions, saying, "My religion is best. The only way to go to God or to heaven is to be a Christian or a Hindu or a Buddhist." I say, all roads lead to Rome. Whatever religion you are following, if you are following it truly, no religion will teach you hatred.

No religion will teach you violence, hatred, anger, conflict, war. Every religion will teach you compassion, love, service, generosity, peace. Therefore, follow your religion, whatever it is, and respect other religions. I would like to see more inter-faith communication and dialogue. In this way, we can have some understanding for each other. So, start with education, go to media and go to religious people. If you can sort out those three dimensions then I think economics, politics, etc., will be following those three leads.

I: Politics comes always afterwards?

Satish: Yes. Politics is a result of people's mindset. The politics, economics, etc. are the result of our minds and our thinking. So, we have to start with our mind and our world view. If we change our world view, then our politics, economics, business, science and technology will follow. Where do we start? We start with education, with media, with inter-religious, inter-faith dialogue.

I: How do you see the role of business in the *Sarvodaya* world or society?

Satish: Business has a place in *Sarvodaya*, but the purpose of business should be to meet the needs of humans and nature, rather than to make money and profit. Making money and profit is not bad, if it is a sub-text, by-product, as long as your motivation and your intention to do business is to exchange goods and services to facilitate life. So, if I am making clothes and you are producing food, a business person will bring my food to you, and your clothes to me. The businessman can be a bridge between the needs of one community and another, or one individual and another. So, business has a good function.

Two great supporters of Mahatma Gandhi were businessmen, (Jamnalal) Bajaj and (Ghanshyam Das) Birla (of the Birla group), both starting with B. So business is not bad in itself, but it is the motivation, the intention that matters. Gandhi created business – the khadi business, the village industries business. In Gandhi's time and after that, for a long time, in every major town there would be a khadi shop (this is diminishing now), and they would sell hand-made cloth and village industry goods, oil, soap, shoes. Gandhi did not oppose business.

But these khadi shops were not owned by individuals, they were owned by communities, trusts or foundations, and no one person was making profit. Everybody who worked in the shop got their livelihood, they were paid. Nobody was not paid. But the shops were owned by the community. In the same way, you can have business which is not for profit-making, personal gain, personal wealth, but for the benefit of the community. And now, even big businesses, which I don't like, have some good points. Tatas are a very big business, international business, but the majority of their shares are in a trust, and that trust (foundation) gives money to good causes. The majority shareholding is by the trust. That is a good model. But Gandhi would say, and I would say, that you have become too big, and you are not wise about what to sell and what to make. You are making cars, steel, have environmentally destructive businesses. Gandhi's business will be business which is sustainable, beautiful and durable, and not damaging to the soil, society, soul and spirit, and is keeping you happy. What kind of business you do (matters) ... If it is not damaging anybody, sociologically just, ecologically sustainable, spiritually fulfilling, it is a good business. So, business can be spiritual if you do it in the right way.

I: I was just wondering what your thoughts are about the European Union ... and how it was established on the premise of acceptance of diversity. Can the European Union transform itself to *Sarvodaya* in the future?

Satish: The European Union started with good intentions. Because, after World War II, it was realised that Europe had been fighting war after war after war. The First World War, and before that the Crimean war, and others. The Germans, French, British ... were all enemies. So they decided that in order to make peace they had to find a way of living together as good neighbours. That was the intention. Originally, they had the Common Market and freedom of movement. There are many good things about the European Union. I voted, and my wife June voted, to remain in the European Union, and not for Brexit. However, I am not an uncritical admirer of the European Union. There are certain things that I think the EU have got wrong. Number one is that they don't care enough and nourish and support small growers, small farmers, small cheese makers, small winemakers.

They bring so many bureaucratic rules – about the machines and conditions for making cheese that make it very expensive. So small cheese makers, small farmers, small producers cannot afford to have such expensive establishments. The EU appears to favour large businesses and large, bureaucratic, mechanised production systems. I don't like that. But I like it that within Europe you can travel without any visa. I don't have to take a visa for France, Spain, Germany or Italy, I can go anywhere, people can move. I prefer that people move rather than goods move.

Brexit means, move the goods, we want your money, we want your goods, we want you to have our goods, we want to have your money, but we don't want your people. That is very divisive, separating. That is not diversity, that is not unity, not *Sarvodaya*. I would say, I want your people, come and stay, bring German music, French plays, Italian opera, bring them. But keep your water in France and we will keep our water in

Scotland. The exchange of water from France to Scotland, that is my favourite example to show we don't want goods to travel so much but people to travel, walking, going slowly or hitch-hiking, taking trains. All the time humanity has moved, we are all immigrants. We all come from Africa, all originally from Africa.

So, this idea that we can stop people travelling is not right ... We went to New Zealand, to Australia. The aboriginal people didn't say you can't come to our country. Are we so low and so mean that we want to stop people coming, or friends, or supporters (from coming to our land). So, I am in favour of an EU-type organisation and I would like to see this even in India. Mahatma Gandhi's great friend and follower Vinoba Bhave used to say, let us make, like EU, the ABC union, A meaning Afghanistan, B meaning Burma, C meaning Ceylon [now Sri Lanka], and make a EU type of unity among these countries. We can travel freely without any visa or passport and have a common market.

I would like EU to be less bureaucratic and less harsh on small business, small producers, small cheese makers, small winemakers and small farmers. If you can support them and keep travel free, and you have goods produced locally, and once you have something special to trade, then trade. Don't trade in things we have, like French milk going to England, and English milk going to France, and butter coming from New Zealand and our butter going to Russia. That kind of business, with unnecessary travel and transportation, all needs fossil fuel. I would like to have people travelling, and people walking. People walking, bicycling, taking trains or buses, and occasionally a few people flying, it is a small amount, it doesn't matter.

But goods transportation is creating a tremendous amount of fossil-fuel use and climate change and global warming. The military use of fossil fuel is colossal. So, if we have peace in the world, and have decentralised *Sarvodaya*, I am not against people travelling.

I: When you introduce new ideas or people in a place that are contrary to what exists, how do you hold on to your culture and tradition and reconcile it with the new?

Satish: The thing is that tradition and culture have to be continuously renewed. You can't become stagnant, fixed, dogmatic - *my* culture, *my* religion, *my* land, *my* country. So, in your mind you think globally, broad and inclusive, and you keep your feet grounded in the soil wherever you live. You have a local economy like *swadeshi*, you have *swaraj**, which is self-government, so you have your local culture, which you embrace, but at the same time you don't become narrow. You are living in Nairobi, that's wonderful, wherever you are. I am living in England now, I love the land there, I love the trees there, I admire the birds. Every time I go out of the house into my garden I say to my wife, 'Look, we are living in a paradise, how wonderful.' So I don't have to be narrow-thinking – I was born in India, in Rajasthan, that's the only country I want to remain in, I want to maintain and protect my culture. *Wherever you are, you are in the landscape of love.* Wherever you are, there are two landscapes, the outer landscape, you love it, and there wherever you are, say, in Nairobi, there is a local economy there, embrace it.

Wherever you are, embrace the local culture

There is a local culture wherever you are. Embrace it. When we were in Wales, we learnt the Welsh language. In England I have learnt the English language, I go to see Shakespeare, I quote Shakespeare. I was talking to Richard Dawkins and I said to him, "Shakespeare said, 'tongues in trees, books in running brooks, sermons in stones, good in everything'". He said, no, that's poetry, that is not science. I said, but if science and poetry get disconnected, where are we? Bring science and poetry together. So, wherever you are, if you are in Kenya, love Kenya, embrace Kenya, enjoy Kenya. In England, enjoy England. If you are coming and living in India, it is a foreign country, doesn't matter, enjoy India.

Mahatma Gandhi's companion, Mrs. Slade*, who we know as Meerabai, [*Mrs. Madeleine Slade (1892–1982), also known in India as Mirabai or Meerabehn, was the daughter of Sir Edmond Slade, a rear admiral in the British Royal Navy. She became a supporter of the Indian independence movement, left her home in England in the 1920s, and worked closely with Mahatma Gandhi*] was from Austria. And she became more Indian than the Indians. She was a great companion of Mahatma Gandhi. So, I don't see that you have to be static, in one place and remain there, stick to your culture, not changing, not moving. That will become stagnant, dogmatic. I want people to be free, they can go where they like. But wherever you are, love that place. So, I would use the local economy in England, I would buy local butter, organic milk. Traditions will all be renewed and reviewed.

I: You were talking about the metal chairs ...

Satish: No, I am not against metal. I am against metal chairs (laughter). I am not against appropriate use of plastic. I am against plastic bottles, plastic bags, but not against plastic cameras. Because that camera you will use for five to ten years, it is not a single-use item. But plastic bags and plastic bottles are used for five minutes and thrown away ... There is more plastic in the oceans than fish.

To get the metal chair you need a deep mine. I have to disturb the earth to get a chair, that is not appropriate. But if you are making something appropriate made of iron, and if you mine carefully ... you might need metal for a camera, fine, but why for a chair. You can use organic, plentiful wood and straw.

I: Who do you think are today's leading thinkers in the world in the area of eco-spirituality?

Satish: Have you come across Joanna Macy's *The Great Turning*? [She talks about 'The Great Turning' as the third revolution. Can be accessed at https://bit.ly/Satish09] She is an eco-spiritual thinker.

I: She has logically argued and presented the concept of *Tatvamasi* ... [*Tatvamasi, a Sanskrit term translated to mean 'That thou art', is considered the kernel of teachings of ancient Indian spiritual texts, offering the view that you are what you seek*].

Satish: Then there is Charles Eisenstein, who wrote *Sacred Economics: Money, Gift, and Society in the Age of Transition*. He also wrote *The More Beautiful World Our Hearts Know is Possible*. He is a very good eco-spiritual thinker. There was Thomas Berry. He is no longer alive. His book is called *The Dream of the Earth*. Wendell Berry, who is not his brother, is also a very good ecological spiritual thinker, a great man. He wrote a book called *The Unsettling of America: Culture and Agriculture*. Then there is Tim Jackson, who wrote *Prosperity Without Growth*, a very good book.

I: You have said that man and woman make the whole, yin and yang make the whole, good and bad make the whole; do you see violence as an inherent part of non-violence, and the two together as giving us the holistic picture of who we are?

Satish: There I will use slightly different language. We say, '*Asato ma sadgamya, tamaso ma jyotir gamya, mrityor ma amrit gamya.*' [One of the most cited and chanted mantras from one of the ancient Indian spiritual texts, the Brihadaranyaka Upanishad, which means: 'Lead me from falsehood to truth, from darkness to light and from mortality to immortality']. In the same spirit I could say, lead me from violence to non-violence. This means that *tamas* – darkness – exists. But we don't promote it. We promote light. But we accept that *tamas* is there, therefore lead me from darkness to light. In the same way, we say violence exists. Animals eat animals. We eat vegetables, that is violence. Inherently, life gives life, life takes life, life sustains life. This is why life is sacred. Because life sacrifices itself to promote and maintain life. So, there is room for violence, but we don't promote violence, we have to minimise violence and maximise non-violence.

Even Mahatma Gandhi said we cannot eliminate violence altogether; we have to accept it. But we should not have intention or motivation to harm. If you have intention to harm someone, they will also have intention to harm you. Do you want to be harmed, damaged, killed? You don't. So, if you don't want to be harmed, do not harm others.

Although we recognise that without violence there is no non-violence and that violence is part of life, we don't maximise, promote, sell, live in darkness, live in death. We say, lead me from death to life. I will die, death is inevitable, you cannot stop death, but we don't promote death, death is inevitable, we recognise it, we accept it, but we say, from death lead me to life. So that is a different metaphor from the male-female metaphor. There, without the female there is no birth, there is no continuity. So male and female is not in the same category as darkness and light or violence and non-violence.

I: We do see a lot of excess in nature. Millions of sperms are produced to fertilise but one egg, and it could be argued that this is overkill. It could also be argued that the guarantee to see that the species continues is this kind of overkill. Almost like the military argument captured in the words 'shock and awe' ... the doctrine that you must overwhelm your enemy if you want to win.

Satish: But they (the United States) didn't win. They overwhelmed Iraq, but they did not win Iraq. So, you cannot apply the nature metaphor in the same way.

I: The millions of sperms ...

Satish: That is different. There are millions of bacteria in our body. Without them our body cannot exist. But that does not mean we have to make millions of bacteria in society. So that is a different metaphor. In our society we need to have better balance. Violence is there and compassion is also there. So, if Colin Powell (or Bush more specifically) wants to win the hearts and minds of Iraqis he would have to go there with gifts, not weapons. They (US) would have won. Saddam Hussein would be their colleague if they had said we will pay you a better price for your oil, we will give you more gifts for this, that and the other, you are our friends, why are you worried, we have no bad designs on you. He will then be your friend. The US have been opposing Iranian governments for the last 60 years, from 1957 or so. They have not won. They are not going to win North Korea by threatening them.

In Vietnam, about 40,000 American soldiers were killed, and America did not win that country. Vietnam is still communist. But Nixon went to China and said, we don't want to overwhelm you, we will talk with you, we will trade with you. You are communist, you can be, we are not going to interfere with you, we want to be your friends. Now America and China are trading partners. Enmity will breed enmity. Friendship will create friendship. As you sow, so shall you reap. That's the karma. So, this idea of Colin Powell was completely wrong, it failed. And there were no weapons of mass destruction in Iran. Colin Powell himself admitted that this was the biggest mistake he made. Nature's metaphor is quite different, nature is not aggressive. There may be millions of sperm...

I: There is a battle between the sperm of one and the sperm of another to take control and to procreate.

Satish: There is no battle. There is a kind of abundance of seeds. There are millions of acorns forming every year on the oak trees in the forest. Only one or two acorns become oak trees. But that is abundance, that is not overwhelming, aggressive. We are here, you use whatever you want to use. Abundance and prosperity are different from overwhelming and violent force. It is not the same thing.

I: But you do not agree with a similar language when it comes to the market economy. There are so many things to choose from...

Satish: If they did not create waste and pollution, no problem. Those acorns do not create a problem, waste or pollution, they go back to the soil and become soil. If all your production became soil again, became air or water again, and the water, soil and air remained clean, there would be no problem.

Abundance of nature is different from excess and waste of industry

I don't mind any abundance. I am not against abundance. I am against waste and pollution. Our industrial system is creating waste and pollution in nature, and stress in humans. We are all stressed. Working day and night, still I am not happy. Why am I working? Whatever money I get, I still want a promotion, I want a bigger salary. People are discontented. The millions of acorns are not discontented. They go back happily to the soil, become the soil and the tree will produce millions of acorns again.

Nature has prosperity in abundance. I favour abundance, prosperity, beauty, comfort, not convenience.

There is a big difference between comfort and convenience. I want to be comfortable in my body and in my house. But convenience is different. Our industrial society is into convenience, not comfort. People are not comfortable, people in New Delhi and Mumbai are not comfortable. They are sitting in traffic jams, they are drinking polluted water from bottles, they are breathing bad air, they are not comfortable. But things are made convenient. Drive a car and you will travel conveniently; you don't have to go by train.

So, we have to move from convenience to comfort, and from waste and pollution to abundance and prosperity. That is why I do not like words like downsizing, low level of prosperity, etc. Language tells us that we are somehow austere. I am not for austerity. I am for prosperity. I don't want people to be unhappy, I want people to enjoy. *Ananda* is our aim, *Sat-Chit-Ananda** [truth, consciousness, bliss]. That people have forgotten.

Centralised systems have not fed the poor

But Nehru said, I can't feed my poor people and I can't clothe them with the Gandhi *charkha** [*the hand spinning wheel that Gandhi used to spin cloth, making it a symbol of self-reliance and to take a stand against British goods*]. He was wrong. The only way to feed people is to give them freedom to grow their food and have land. The only way to clothe them is to give them the *charkha*, and not make them dependent on Mumbai, Delhi,

Kolkata, London and New York in the globalised economy. After 70 years of independence Indians still do not have enough food and clothes ... There are still millions of people without food.

So, Nehru's opinion that Gandhi's idea of small village economies would not feed and clothe everyone, that India needed large industries and a globalised system for this, proved wrong in 70 years of history.

I: But he said there is landless labour, the people don't have land. What do they do?

Satish: Give them land, there is plenty of land in India. Every family should have two acres. And no factory farming, no need of tractors. Keep your factory farms and tractors or machines, to make machines. I don't mind computers being made by machine, or by robots even. But don't put robots in agriculture, hospitals and schools. Machine making machine is ok. But organic things should not be made by machine.

I: Machines interfering in life...

Satish: Exactly. And if you have technology to aid the human hand, that is good technology, as you are aiding, like a tool. But if you replace hands and make humans redundant, that is bad technology. Gandhi was not against technology and I am not against technology. Gandhiji said, I am delighted that Singer (sewing) machines are being produced. He said the bicycle is good technology. Ivan Illich wrote the books *The Village*, *Deschooling Society, Energy and Equity, Medical Nemesis*. He was a radical Gandhian. So, Gandhi and I, Illich, Schumacher and Herman Daley all are for prosperity, for abundance, for comfort, for the good life ... and that will happen when you dignify work. Schumacher wrote a book called *Good Work*. Work is good in itself. Work is not only to produce goods but work is to express your creativity and imagination. Work is service, it is meditation.

Now, work has become a chore, a drudgery. The industrial society turns what is meditation and intrinsic value into tragedy. Gandhi said, spin the spinning wheel and see the thread, the cotton or wool becoming thread, it is a manifestation of *Ishwar*, the Lord. That thread is a kind of meditation, and the by-product is a shawl. That is a beautiful way of looking at the world. Whereas our thought process in the industrial consumer society has become ugly, putting us down at a lower level of existence. We are not going higher, we are going to a lower level of existence. We may have a lot of clothes and a lot of computers, cars, but humanity is going down. I want to lift humanity, let the cars and computers go down. If cars and computers can help humanity then I am happy. If they cannot...

Humanity, earth, nature, are primary, and technology, science, politics, banks, business ... they are the icing on the cake. But if you have no cake and you eat only icing, you will be ill. This society has too much sugar, and no substance.

I: How long do you think it will be before this message hits home, and 'The Great Turning' in Joanna Macy's description comes to fruition?

Satish: People are becoming aware and realising it, we are already making a journey, but it is impossible to predict when the turning will be. We did not know when the Berlin wall would come down. The CIA did not know. It was like water rising. When the turning point comes, the water will flood, the dam will burst. That is how the Berlin wall came down.

In America, there is still a lot of racial discrimination, nevertheless, white men voted for a black man to be in the White House. Women's liberation – a lot of changes have taken place since Gandhi promoted feminist equality of women and promoted Sarojini Naidu [*1879-1949, Indian political activist, and the first woman to become President of the Indian National Congress*] and many other freedom fighters. Now look at women's liberation all over the world. We have to be part of the solution, not a part of the problem. So we are working for a good, prosperous, wonderful, beautiful society. When it will happen, how it will happen, the results are not in our hands.

Keep going, even if it means walking alone

That is why the ancient wisdom of India is karma or *purushartha**... Never think I do not have to work. Never think that my activism is no good. That I am not going to succeed. And that society is going downhill. Even if society is going downhill, up to your last breath you do not say, I am not going to work. Never wish to have no action. I will remain an activist until the last breath of my life.

Gandhi was an activist till his last breath. Jesus Christ was an activist till the last breath of his life. Those who started the feminist movement did not know when change would happen. Martin Luther King died before he saw that black people could vote, or black people could go to the White

House or the Senate. We do not know. This is not in our hands. This is in the hands of the universe, in the hands of God and circumstances we cannot control. But we will be part of that journey of transformation. We are happy to be activists. We are not hankering and anxious about our success. So, don't worry if society is not listening to you. You carry on. *Ekla cholo re* – walk alone. Keep going and people will come with you.

When Mahatma Gandhi started his salt march from Sabarmati Ashram, he had handpicked 79 *satyagrahis*. Only 10-15 people from the ashram joined him. And then, many people came. And by the end, when he arrived at Dandi, how many people were there? Thousands, 10,000, perhaps. So, you don't worry. You start what you believe in. You put yourself on the line. What will happen, we don't know, we cannot control. So, I don't worry about when society will change, it is not for me to control. I am not the dictator of the world. I am only the servant of the world. I do my best.

I: How do you analyse the situation in India today? There is an industrial paradigm that we are adopting, and our stated, admitted, announced goal is to see that growth goes up, and every time that growth as measured by the Gross Domestic Product, GDP, goes down, there is nervousness. Right now, we have had loud opposition to the current government because growth has gone down.

Satish: So, what is the growth now?

I: GDP at about 5.7%. It fell from about 7%. India, particularly since liberalisation (beginning 1991), has been looking at growth as a means to generate employment, to fight poverty. But human beings are being replaced by robots, 3D printers, artificial intelligence, bots.

Satish: The Congress party or the other parties don't have another better vision. They have the same vision of economic growth as the BJP. Communists want the same economic growth as capitalists. The state will do it or private industry will do it ... the goal is the same. So my view is that if you are using technology or machines to make machines on a limited scale, without waste and pollution, and with durability and all the other aspects we have talked about, that is acceptable. That is acceptable as long as organic work, service, teaching, hospital work, farming, manufacturing of clothes, shoes, furniture, all organic things, are done by hand. And measurement (of prosperity) should be like in Bhutan where they talk about Gross National Happiness not Gross National Product.

I think Bhutan could be a good example for the rest of the world, a small country with a big idea. So, India can be humble and learn from Bhutan, and say that India's goal is not Gross National Product but Gross National Happiness. We will share before we continue to grow, we must share more.

I: There is a question of giving alms versus having a dignified livelihood.

Satish: I support dignified livelihood. People should have work where they live and not have to move to find work. Work should be brought to the people, not the people to the work. So, work should be brought to villages; and arts, crafts and agriculture should be as important as banking, business and machines.

India is poor because it has no love, no sharing

Satish: Arts, crafts and agriculture – these are the three things that will provide millions of jobs. But India is not poor because it has no money – India is poor because it has no love.

We have to have a different world view. The Modi government and the BJP are not pursuing the Hindu spirit. They might be pursuing Hindu nationalism, Hindu ritualism and Hindu institutionalism, but they are not pursuing the Hindu spirit. The Hindu spirit is to go for humanity, service, caring, sharing ... those are the values. Then pragmatism will follow.

I: They are giving Hinduism a bad name.

Satish: Yes, they are. So, pragmatism should follow idealism. Money should follow service. Money will come. Go to Tirupati [*a pilgrimage centre in India's Andhra Pradesh state, where the world's richest temple, the Venkateshwara temple, is located*]. Is there shortage of money there? They don't ask for anything, you can go for free. You don't have to give a penny. But people put money. They have so much money they are starting hospitals and schools and still they don't know what to do with their money. There is no shortage of money. The government of India can give every citizen of India enough to live properly. Money is only an idea. One day Modi decides that all that old money should go, and new money is coming. There was some difficulty but money came. In England, there was a shortage of money and [with quantitative easing] they created billions out of thin air. They printed paper money. So, money is there, it is not a problem.

Joyful livelihoods versus soulless jobs

When we have arts, crafts and agriculture, the artists, craftsmen and farmers have jobs, those are the forms of livelihood. I don't like the words 'jobs', 'unemployment' ... I call it livelihood. Because I want people to do work with freedom and joy, and that is not a job. If you want to do something, you do it because you love it. Love what you do, and do what you love. So, if we can create that distinction, between where to use machines and where not to use machines, then I think we can create a better balance.

I: You have been out of India for 45 years. Have you been an India watcher, do you track political and economic developments here?

Satish: Not enough. I come to India every year, I have been coming for about 13 years. I also go to Bengaluru, to a place called Bhoomi College, which promotes ecological living and was started by Seetha Ananthasivan. I also visit the Gnostic Centre in Delhi, set up as a prototype of the universities of tomorrow. So I visit two or three places. The Gnostic Centre has been set up by Amita Mehra who has been inspired by Shri Aurobindo [*(1872-1950), Indian nationalist, poet and philosopher*]. The centre works to build spiritual and ecological consciousness among people.

I: I wanted to talk to you about the simple practical example of dairy.

Milk is celebrated in the Indian context as a healthy, desirable and sacred food. But dairy production is of a kind that is not ecologically friendly and certainly not using animal-friendly methods. Do you think that by consuming milk, you and I are in some sense supporting this industry? Is veganism the way to go?

SATISH: I urge people not to drink milk in the West, and I avoid it as much as I can. I am not a vegan, but I generally avoid milk products in England because of the factory farming. In India the tradition ... my mother kept cows ... so that is a different culture. Having a cow at home as part of your agricultural economy, where the bullock is ploughing and the cow dung is your compost, and whatever small amount of milk is left after feeding the calf, you use it as icing on the cake, a small amount of milk. That is a totally different concept from this mass-produced milk at a cheap price but at an expensive cost to nature.

I: But that milk that you talk about will not reach everyone.

Satish: You don't need it to reach everywhere.

I: You would be without milk in the cities.

Satish: But in cities a few decades back ... in Mumbai, milk came from cows and buffaloes not far away. Thirty years ago, there were areas in Mumbai with dairy farms where the cows were hand-milked and they were looked after. The city should not grow to more than one or two million people. We do not want to maintain the kind of urban culture we have today of 20 to 40 million people.

If you want fresh milk, live in the country

Mexico City has a population of 40 million, Mumbai and Delhi are growing. And you want all the facilities of nature and the country in the city. That's not possible. If you want nice fresh milk, live in the country. What is so attractive in Delhi? So, you want to have your cake and eat it too. You either have your cake on your table or in your stomach, but you can't have it both ways.

So, if you want milk, each small city should have a 20-30-50-mile radius preserved, conserved, protected, for agricultural produce for that city. Milk, grain and vegetables should come from within that area, a protected green area with not too much construction. Within the city you can have some areas with grass fields, you can have a nice green city. On the roof and on the walls of your buildings you must grow some vegetables. The roof should have solar panels, and for water conservation, every roof must collect water. You can have a sensible design for a city.

At the moment there is no sensible design of cities. Cities are not made for sustainability, nor for food. Craftsmen and arts are all gone, so all that remains in cities is bureaucracy, offices and banks and business – those are the main, and other things are peripheral. I would like to have a new urban design and planning where nature and culture are married, they live side by side, with no contradiction between them. At the moment, we have exiled nature, and have factory farming. That is not nature. We have lost common sense. Common sense is that your food, without which we can't live, must be as close, fresh and healthy as possible. If we cannot maintain that, where is our intelligence, science, wisdom? Food is basic, and we have spoilt the food, made sugary and salty food and imported, packaged and processed food – that is tragic. So we have to work towards a new urban design and planning.

I: Is there scope for agriculture today to feed billions of people? The trend is that by 2030 India could be 40% urban and by 2050, 50% or 60% urban. I am not saying this should reverse, but how do we check this rush of urban growth? Do you see any hope from what is happening elsewhere, maybe in Europe? What is the viability of an urban unit from the point of view of producing 'roti kapda aur makaan' – food, clothing and shelter?

Satish: In England – also in Europe – there are two or three strong movements. One is 'Back to the Land'. Many people, highly educated, urban people, are leaving the cities and starting self-sufficient, small-scale, 10-acre to 20-acre farms. That is a big movement. And there is a lot of flow from the city to the countryside. Second, there is a tremendous growth in gardening. The permaculture movement is strong, and also agro-economy culture and organic gardening. Even on television, there is Monty Don who has an organic gardening programme on BBC ('Gardeners' World'). The third big movement is urban farming. I was visiting a friend near Oxford Street in the heart of London, and he asked me if I would like to see his garden. I said, 'A garden, here in London?' We went up the stairs, and on the roof there was a beautiful garden, and honey bees. He gave me a pot of honey. 'I made this honey from this bee-hive, here.' He was growing vegetables, flowers, herbs like thyme, sage and rosemary, tomatoes, heather and flowers so that the honey bees can make honey. That was an example. There are many roof gardens and wall gardens in London.

So there is a start, still in the minority, but there is a strong minority, growing, interested in gardening, roof and wall gardening and the 'Back to the Land' movement, small-scale, self-sufficient. How far it will go, when it will change (into a major trend), we don't know, but it is a good movement.

I: One of India's major problems is that people are not leaving villages for want of food. Push migration, which happens because of destitution, seems to be coming down and pull migration, which is aspirational, seems to be going up. How do we really reverse this?

Satish: The pull of money. You get more money when you are in the city. With more money you can buy things which are consumer attractions. In rural areas, you may have food and the basics, but you don't have money.

I: Your self-worth goes up, your worth in society goes up. You get a better bride or groom.

Satish: So, what we need to do is to change the culture, the way of thinking that money is more important than a good way of life. How we do it is difficult, because the value society gives to money and consumerism and glamour is more than to land, nature and gracious living. So, from gracious living to glamorous living is the present trend. Turning that around, from glamorous to gracious living, is a big challenge. So we have to bring (to these rural places) a good, comfortable, prosperous – but not extravagant and wasteful – life, and more work, arts, crafts, agriculture. Those things have to be made more attractive and also more financially rewarding. That is the only way. Otherwise young people want to go to school, then university, and then get a job in a city.

I: Those who can't go to university are also moving towards cities. When I [Sudarshan Iyengar] was growing up in Kachchh, it was aspiration-based pull-migration towards Mumbai for most Gujaratis. And there are two words we use – *desh* and *watan* [referring to one's native places in Kachchh]. So you still had this concept of going back to your roots (of returning at some point in your life or sending money home). It is no longer there with this generation. But there was a system in that the urban economy supported the rural by means of what used to be the "money order" service of the India postal department.

Satish: My family, my brothers and father, would go to Assam, Bihar or Bengal for business – jute. They would have houses there but they always came back in the rainy season. They had their *havelis* (traditional, often palatial houses or mansions) in Rajasthan and the family lived there, the children grew up there, so they maintained two houses. Even if the wives and mothers went with them, some servants or some people would look after the *haveli*. Even now you can go to my village, my brothers and sisters are still there.

I: Which is your village?

Satish: It is not quite a village, it is quite a big town – Shri Dungargarh, between Bikaner and Jaipur. The *havelis* are still there. Their owners earned money in Bengal or Bihar or Calcutta and brought the money to build the house, for weddings, for all the ceremonies and festivals. They spent the money locally. So there was a kind of balance. Nowadays, young people want to sell their family house and go and live in Mumbai, go with the times. 'Where do you come from?' 'I come from Mumbai.' They do not want to declare that they are from Kachchh or Rajasthan.

But the future in my view lies in promoting our arts, crafts and agriculture. That should be the basis of the economy, and everything else, like technology and science, banking, other economic activities and services, should be to support it. If we can have 50% or 60% of our economy based on arts, crafts, making things, manufacturing things ... people will have work.

I: How do you change this mindset? All that you are talking about, agriculture, working with the soil, working with the hands, is basically seen as drudgery.

Satish: Working in a bank or office for 20-30 years of your life ... is it a life of less drudgery? Commuting every day to the city in a bus or train, in Mumbai or wherever ... less drudgery? Sitting in a car, less drudgery? This is a mindset, it is an idea that working on the land is drudgery, but that in an office is not. It is as much drudgery, sometimes more. But people like it.

Do you know that Jain story? There was somebody who was in the forest and he met two wild elephants. In order to escape them he climbed a tree and went up a branch. Then the two elephants surrounded the tree with their trunks and shook it. A bee hive on the tree got disturbed and the bees came out and started to sting this man who was hanging from the tree. But there was a drop of honey coming his way. An angel was coming by, in a *pushpa-viman* [an aeroplane] and saw this man's predicament, and asked, "Do you want help, can we rescue you? The tree will go down and you are being stung by bees." He said, "Yes, please help me, but can you wait for one minute for this drop of honey." The drop came and then another minute passed. He was being stung, he was in danger, but he was not leaving, and the angel went away and he died. So, at the moment, money is honey, this little drop of honey of consumerism.

Life in cities is not that comfortable. I lived in London for many years and I had to move out of London and went to a little village of 1,000 people in the south-west, in Devon, Hartland. Now when I go to the city, I find it too much. The amount of money you have to spend in the city, on taxis and food ... and everything is more expensive.

I: It is the same in India.

CHAPTER 11:

Money Making Money: The destructive business model

The shareholder model of business is outdated but it still rules many aspects of the world. Satish Kumar is firmly anti-capitalist. He makes a clear distinction between a free market – a useful platform for buying and selling of goods and services – and the stock market, which he says is simply the unethical practice of money making more money.

There are new business models being experimented with, an often-cited example being Triodos Bank. Paul Polman, who was CEO of the old corporate giant Unilever from 2009 to 2019, was a poster boy of business sustainability. Unilever is essentially a giant marketing company, their wares manufactured by somebody else but branded and marketed by them. They have begun to say they are committed to source goods from ecological sources. New investments would also mean more money in advertising to maintain market share.

But Satish Kumar feels that big will bring with it all the attendant problems of big.

I: Are you supportive of or sceptical about the efforts of large companies like Unilever attempting to become more ecologically sensitive?

Satish: When a big business like Unilever takes such steps towards sustainability, that means the ecological movement is making some impact on mainstream society. I would say this is a good thing. But if you take the whole system, rather than just partially (there is a book by Fritjof Capra and Pier Luigi Luisi, *The Systems View of Life: A Unifying Vision)*, anything that is so big can never be sustainable. Ultimately, they have to sustain the business rather than sustain nature.

Triodos Bank is different. I bank with them. It is small scale and more decentralised and is using money for good purposes, whereas Unilever's ultimate aim is to make money and not necessarily serve society. Serving society has become a means to the end of making money. But Triodos Bank is using money as a means to serve society as an end, so it is a completely different model. If Unilever says we will make ourselves carbon neutral that is good as far as it goes, but not far enough from the point of view of ecological economics or environmental sustainability or the Earth. They should say that they are here not to make profit, profit is only a by-product; they should say they are here to ensure everything they make is recycled, re-absorbed, biodegradable, i.e., a cyclical economy. If they can say that they are moving from a linear economy to a cyclical economy, I would consider that a stronger step.

I: The shareholder model of business must collapse?

Satish: It must go. It is completely living on money, not on labour, work, creativity or imagination, just on your money. Money making money. Today you put 100,000 rupees in the bank or in shares of Unilever or any big business for that amount to become 150,000 or 200,000 rupees. So you are always making money from money.

I: A capitalist may argue, where is the money going to come from to run enterprises to serve the people in distant corners of the globe the way they do now. In the Indira Gandhi era in India, soap was not available, you had to fix the price of soap, and the government came into the picture to control it. As a result, soap disappeared. So capitalists would argue, where would the money to manufacture for or provide services to millions of people come from?

Satish: Soap was not disappearing because there was no money, but because people were not making soap. If you make soap in exchange for money, money is only an idea, coming from your computer or your brain. It is not a real substance but only a concept. Today I say I am transferring 100,000 rupees from my bank into your bank. It is only an idea, a figure.

I: A diary entry.

Satish: Yes, a diary entry. It is not a substance, but soap is real. You make and I take. And there is an exchange. I make shoes and you take them. Instead of I having shoes for you and you having soap for me, we have this good idea of money to make exchange of goods easy. Money is a good invention as a means of exchange. But when it is not a means of exchange

... when soap is to make money, and money to make soap, that is capitalism and exploitation. If you don't have money, you don't have soap.

I: So you are anti-capitalist?

Satish: I am an anti-capitalist.

I: Are you negating the market?

Satish: I am negating capitalism, not the market. They are not the same. The market is a free market where you bring your things, I bring my things, we sit in the market, we exchange, people come and buy and sell. A free market is not the same thing as the stock market. As with 'science' and 'sustainability', the meaning of 'market' is also distorted. A market is where people bring things and buy and sell them. The stock market is what I am opposed to, not the free market.

I: That is a good distinction. The existence of the market has come about because of the complexity of the system. We progressed from barter because it became difficult to barter. As we went on making the systems more complex, price was the signal to which the producer responded.

Satish: Price is not the problem. The problem is money making money. Capitalism is not about price, it is about capital making capital. And capital has no value to make capital. That is completely exploitative. If you say you are in the market today, there are a lot of shoes but no soap. So the value of soap can go up. If the demand is more you pay a bit more. That is ok. But if you say, I have 100 rupees, which I will give you, and after a month you give me 150 rupees, that is rupees making rupees, that is capitalism. Before capitalism, industrialisation, materialism, we had the market, even if we did not have rupees. The medium of exchange is not a problem, it is the means to an end. The end is to exchange, to serve, to look after each other's needs, respect skills. Work is good in itself.

I: How do you reward services? The medium of exchange is not only convenient for exchanging goods, you require it for services...

Satish: You have a gift economy. The Brahmin comes to serve a wedding and he gets a gift. A musician like Ravi Shankar plays and we applaud him and give him a gift – that is the gift economy in services and exchange of actual goods. And it has worked for many years. How do priests and saints get money? They don't need money, they need gifts. I lived for nine years as a monk. How did I live? I was not producing food, clothes, shoes, or anything. I was teaching and people gave me gifts, *dana*. So, the gift economy is an essential part of the free market.

I: That kind of a low-level equilibrium economy...

Satish: I would call it the proper economy.

I: Maybe this economy you suggest can sustain only a limited number of people on this Earth. Hayek argues that it is the industrial revolution which could really sustain what you call the poor. Capitalism, with its economies of scale, can produce at such cheap rates that you can provide goods and services to a large number of people for their survival.

Satish: You produce so much that companies are now burning hundreds of tons of clothes because they cannot sell them. In every season, if you go to Oxford Street or to any shopping area in a Western city, the second-hand shops are full of goods they want to send to Africa. The Africans say they do not want so much, your second-hand clothing is destroying our local industry, local design and clothes production. We produce so much that it is superfluous. The machine is so hungry it wants work for twenty-four hours, and people are so hungry for money they want to produce more to make more money. It has ruined our society. It has not succeeded.

People who innovated – Newton and Darwin, for instance – were not paid for their innovation, Buddha and Jesus Christ were not paid for their work. Innovation is always imaginative work. Shakespeare was not paid to write his plays, he did not have a copyright, but he wrote because he was a poet. Kalidas [*Indian classical poet and scholar, noted for his plays and considered one of the greatest Indian poets, 5th century CE*] was not paid. Innovation has nothing to do with money. Innovation is a spiritual, imaginative and idealistic activity, you do it for the pleasure of doing it.

Tulsidas wrote the whole of the *Ramayana* ... "For my own delight and pleasure I write the Tulsi Ramayana", he wrote. I am working all my life editing a magazine, not for money. I am sitting with you, I am giving you my service, how much are you going to pay me? That is a very low level of coming down to for your imagination to be sold for hundred rupees or more.

The highest level of innovation is for pleasure, for joy. I am happy to write a book and I am happy that you read it, I am happy to see you write poetry and I am happy to read it. Ravi Shankar is not playing for money, he is playing for joy. So, this idea that innovation and services have to be paid for and measured in money, that is completely bringing humanity down. That is not the economy of nature.

There are five hundred mango trees, each producing hundreds of mangoes, not because they want money from you but for their pleasure. They are happy ... spring has come, the blossoms have come, the fruit is here and I am here for you, come enjoy the mangoes. The mango tree will never ask you where your VISA card is, how much money have you got, how rich you are, and that if you don't have a hundred rupees you won't have mangoes. Tulsidas will never say you can hear my *Ramayana* only if you have money, come and listen to me. If we reduce that aspect of society, of joy and pleasure and contribution and exchange and give and take, we are destroying our society and culture. This is what science, technology, industrialism, capitalism and consumerism are doing ... destroying human culture.

I: Culture not only holds the past but is also what evolves.

Satish: There is *sanskriti* – culture – and there is *vikruti* – perversion. To some extent, consumerism is *vikruti*, not *sanskriti*. It is not culture, it is civilisation. I would say civilisation is different from culture. Civilisation relates to civic and city. But culture is related to land and cultivating, it is part of the soil and comes from nature. Nature and culture are complementary.

I: How would you explain population, the human species number, which has taken a sudden sharp turn upwards...

Satish: The human population has gone sharply upwards with the same speed and the same level as industrialisation. Pre-industrial societies did not have population problems. The population problem is a result of industrialism.

I: And that is claimed as a positive achievement.

Satish: But now, if there are more and more people who consume more and more, if everybody lived like the USA or Japan, we would need three planets, and we have only one.

I: Gandhi said that in 1930.

Satish: If Britain, in order to get where it is, it had to colonise half the world, how many colonies will India need.

I: If you say you don't want such a society, is it not an ethical point that you are going to stop the arrival and sustenance of a large number of the human species? You may call this an anthropocentric argument. But suppose you go the ecosystems way, then space for the human species will also be limited by the constraints imposed by nature. Is this a tenable argument, and how would you respond to this?

Satish: My response is that nature and culture go together, they are complementary. In that culture, caring and innovation, care for the child and the health of the mother are ethically and culturally right. We do not have to follow the Western system. We can have doctors and traditional midwives. Good care of babies and reduction of maternal and infant mortality – I accept it is culturally and ethically correct. But I don't accept this idea that everybody has to live as long as they can, the idea of keeping everybody alive at any cost – I do not accept that as ethical. I say, live as long as you can live happily and healthily. If you die at 60 or 70, it is better to die a natural death. I am ready to die at any time. I don't want to live very long with science and technology making me live longer. What is wrong with dying? Death is as welcome as birth. Birth should be healthy, peaceful, without danger of unnecessary death of the baby or the mother. That I accept is an ethical and cultural dimension. But I don't accept the idea of keeping everyone alive for as long as possible.

I: So all that is being done to control hypertension, diabetes, and all the research that goes on, do you think it should be stopped and that a person who is not healthy in some normal sense should be allowed to go away?

Satish: I would say that many health problems are the result of the industrial system and our way of life. So however much medical research you do, you are not reducing illness. The British government spends billions on health – you can see it in the NHS budget. But still, if you want to go to a doctor for surgery you have to wait eight weeks. If you think that money and innovation can solve the problem, then look at the reality.

I: The epidemiological studies tell us that compared with the last century, longevity has improved.

Satish: Illness has not decreased in the present time. Now people are living longer but living unhealthy lives. Because what we eat, what we breathe, are all polluted. Water in plastic bottles is not healthy, junk food is not healthy. First you make money to create problems, then you make money to solve problems. In any shop in London, the first window will have junk food – sweets, chocolates and rubbish, things in plastic packets. But never is real, fresh food available in any supermarket.

And if you go to a little corner selling organic food it will be twice as expensive. The system, the way of life, is so mad and so stupid that you think that by having more and more medical research, for which you pay billions to all the medical and pharmaceutical companies, you will solve your health problems. You are living in a cloud. Health is natural, you live a healthy life. Diseases may come but you will find a cure – ayurvedic, herbal.

I: Creating unhealthy lifestyles and finding solutions to their ill-effects is certainly bad. But hasn't science controlled influenza, plague and cholera, and improved child survival? I was a sick child and my mother could not nurse me well, but I survived because even then, in the fifties, there was a good enough medical system to see that I didn't die. Now the ethical question is, do we say that if the species that comes into this world is not hardy enough to survive, it has no reason to and nature does not mourn it?

Satish: The problem is that ethics apply throughout our lives, and not with respect to just one or two things. If our food is produced and distributed unethically, if we are treating nature unethically and all our things are unethical ... and only one or two things, like action on childbirth and plague, will make it all ethical, and we will also make a lot of profit from that ethical step ... that is inconsistent. We have to see the whole picture.

Holistic thinking is about how we live in a way that is healthy and 100% ethical and spiritual. I live with compassion in my heart, love and non-violence are my mottos. I am 100% wedded to ethical points, but not selectively. At the moment our society uses the argument of ethics selectively, but ultimately they want to make money with their ethical arguments.

If Monsanto, for example, said they were so driven about saving the world, feeding the people, that they offered a free service for improved seeds, for people to use if they wanted to, that would be ethical. But why does Monsanto want to make billions of dollars by controlling genetically engineered seeds in the name of feeding the world? Ethics with profit and capitalism mixed together is a fatal mix. If you are really ethical, Monsanto, if you really want to save the world and feed the world, give your seeds free of charge as a service, and we will give you whatever we think proper in exchange. And thank you. Monsanto, what a great thing you have done, here is a present for you, 100 rupees or 1,000 rupees or a million.

The corporate world of selective ethics

Medical pharmaceutical companies are using the argument of medical ethics, but it is a fake argument. Ethics is not selective, ethics is total, a complete picture. The side effects of modern medicine are so lethal, where is the ethics there? If you take herbal or ayurvedic medicine, exercise and take rest, you work, you are not worried, you have no tensions, you live a good life, then that is an ethical life. Now there is no value accorded to work or exercise or living in nature. We are living in congested cities with polluted air, and they will give you medicine. That is not ethics, that is profiteering, capitalism in the name of ethics. So, I think we need to see the whole picture.

I: If Monsanto had said we will give you the seeds free and a pharma company said take medicines for free, then where will the money come from for investment in the research and technology required to develop the seeds and medicines?

Satish: We will give you, when we have seen that the new innovation is good. Where did Buddhists get money to build all their temples, and Christians to build churches; where did Shakespeare get money to print millions of copies of his works? This happens, society will give you. Money is not an entity in short supply, there is no end of it floating around in the world. You can't count how much there is, trillions going around every minute, just chasing more money. Money is only an idea. Monsanto will be absolutely fine, like the Buddhist and Christian church, Hindu temples. Monsanto will have lots of temples and we will worship that. You are a Buddha, you saved our world, have fed the world, so we will worship you. You don't need to bargain. If you are driven by love, and you bargain, that is not love, not ethics, not philanthropy. If Monsanto tells you what you must do in order for the company to invest, then you already have done something unethical. Tulsidas did not say how will I get money to write my book. He said I'll write it. Shakespeare, Beethoven, Bach, Ravi Shankar did not ask how they would get money. They gave. That is ethics, that is love, it is not violence. Money is nothing, there is no short supply of money, believe me. I have lived eighty-one years and I tell you there is no shortage of money in the world. There is a shortage of sharing, caring, ethics, idealism, love, but no shortage of money.

I: Going back to your idea of sustainability, do you think that the whole economy has to be downscaled...

Satish: No, it should be brought to an appropriate scale.

I: So, is appropriate lower than it is now? How do we really resolve this?

Satish: We must produce goods that have three qualities. They should be beautiful. The modern industrial system creates ugliness. You drive from Dehradun station to here, there is not a single beautiful house. So, everything we make should be beautiful. If it is made by hand, by imagination, by humans, it will be beautiful. It is not down-sizing, it is not bringing down. That is not the language I want to use. It should be beautiful. Bring up your economy. I want upscaling not downscaling, but upscale in quality, beauty. Then, whatever you make beautiful should also be useful. Your pots, shoes, chairs, tables, house, food ... all should be beautiful and also useful. Usefulness is as essential as beauty. The third principle is it should be durable. When this computer is made, they should give you guarantee for twenty years. And after twenty years they should make such a computer that it is a complete revolution. It should last you for life. Shoes should last for ten years. Why should clothes be discarded every season? Because of fashion? There is no durability in society.

I call it the BUD principle – beautiful, useful, durable. I am not talking about down-sizing, I am talking about upsizing. I believe the level, standard and quality should go up. At the moment our industrial, mechanised, materialistic consumer society is bringing us down in the true sense. So I don't accept this downscaling language. I believe in upscaling. Regarding railway stations, Prince Charles says that in the olden days, we built our railway stations to look like libraries. Nowadays we make our libraries look like railway stations. I agree. Our industrial system of production is producing ugly, useless, non-durable, unsustainable products which we have to burn when we can't sell them, or put in a landfill. You go to the rubbish heaps in England or America, you see beautiful clothes, lovely usable things, thrown away, as they have too much. We are producing too much, but it is ugly and unsustainable. So, I am talking about upsizing, not downsizing.

I: This is an entirely new system you are envisaging, and the current economy must then be burnt down for the new to be built. That is an extremist view and a violent view.

Satish: It is not extremist. Within the old shell, new will grow. Within the old system that we have today, we can't have a new slate, a clean slate. We have to live in the system we are in by constructing what Gandhi called the creative programme. Create alternatives, create Schumacher College, create Gujarat Vidyapith, organic farming, within the existing system. We can't just dream of another system and have it appear tomorrow. We have to start creating alternative systems, and then, when the old system runs down, let it run down. Then these organic farms and holistic schools and colleges will come up. Then they will run down as well and some new ones will emerge. So, you have to continuously renew your spirit and your organisations and structures. So, renewal and regeneration is what I am advocating. Continuous renewal.

We have to work on creating an alternative constructive programme, what Gandhi called *rachanatmak kaaryakram*. You resist, you critique the old system. But that is not enough – you have to build a new system and those two go together.

In my book *No Destination,* I interpret the eleven principles of Gandhi for our times, following more ecological and holistic paradigms.

Take the principle of non-violence. I extend non-violence to nature, which in Gandhian times they did not seek or teach too much, or think so much about. Even *Sarvodaya* I take much further than many Gandhians did. I say *Sarvodaya* includes forests, animals, rivers, mountains, insects, wildlife, everything. I teach everyone, *Sarvey bhavan tu sukhinah [a mantra from the Upanishads that says: may everyone be at peace* – so, '*sarvey*' includes humans and other-than-humans. I bring in the spiritual, sociological and ecological trinity – that is my Gandhian interpretation.

I: How do you see Amartya Sen's intervention in the debate among the economists in these matters. He seems to steer clear of – or does not have much consciousness about – the issue of ecology.

Satish: Yes, he leaves it out. He has more of a Nehruvian consciousness. And he comes from a socialist and left-thinking background. For him humans are the goal and purpose, and human wellbeing ... anthropocentric. I like his idea of development as freedom and that book [*Development as Freedom*] was very good. Development is not just economic development, it is also freedom, people being able to decide how they will live. But he doesn't include ecological-environmental. I have met him and mentioned this to him. He said that he was born in Shanti Niketan* and Gurudev Tagore always talked about nature, but somehow his passionate concern is more for humans.

I: To not consider nature as an essential and integral part of the human species ... is this arrogance, incidentally? Also, there is a good deal of controversy and disagreement on the various claims and counter-claims on climate change variables. Nobody agrees.

Satish: There is a very large consensus among scientists and in the Paris agreement, where 195 nations agreed that climate change is a real issue and that it is caused by human activities. Though there are still sceptics, like Trump, and others. But I would say it is less controversial now than it used to be. The Kyoto protocol has still quite a lot of controversy, Copenhagen more or less failed. But in Paris, there was more consensus.

There is a more sustainable way to live

It is the way of life, the way of living, with which I am more concerned, which has to be joyful, beautiful, enjoyable, and also sustainable, from the point of view of nature's limits. If we have no *sanyam* – no restraint, no limits – it will be like a river whose banks are broken. Then it is no longer a river, it is a flood. The flood is not going to sustain anybody.

If we forget this idea of limits, then what we are facing is global warming, climate change and many other problems. The issue is, ultimately what kind of sustainable life you want to live so that your economy is sustainable for not only a hundred or five hundred years, but for millennia.

I: So all these wonders that the human species has achieved – reaching Mars and the moon, sending satellites into space, etc., do you see this as a deviation, something unsustainable? Is the species headed for its own destruction?

Satish: I would like to ask why these things are being done. Is it for name, for fame, prestige, human glory, for the collective ego?

I: Curiosity and exploration, to know the unknown, to go beyond, go where we have never gone.

Satish: Curiosity should have some purpose. That purpose is so expensive. When people have no food, even in America, when they do not have medicines, even in Russia ... In Russia all people are not well and happy, they have no food, no housing, and they are going on space travel, for curiosity. It is out of proportion. And what you are actually saying to me is that we have made a mess of this world, now we are going to make a mess of the moon and Mars and colonise there. This is not pure curiosity and exploration. The American government, Russian government, Indian government are funding all this, not for pure curiosity and adventure. They are funding because they want to get resources, control, prestige and power. I am bigger than you, stronger than you, I can go to space ... macho ... not principle, not spiritual, not ecological. So I don't subscribe to this space travel and colonising of the moon and Mars.

I: No species worries about its fellow species for their survival. The stronger ones survive and the weaklings disappear.

Satish: That is not the case. That's totally wrong philosophy and science. The reality of the world is that earthworms have not disappeared, butterflies have not disappeared.

I: I am talking about individuals within the same species.

Satish: Lions don't eat lions, tigers don't eat tigers, elephants don't hunt elephants...

I: Male lions kill the cubs from another male lion once they take over a new pride. Quite a few species eat their own offspring. The larger question is, they don't bother about a weakling among them or care for it. The weak one will die and the stronger ones will survive.

Satish: It may be an exception that lions kill lions, I don't know about it, I am not an expert on species. The majority of nature survives on co-operation and not on competition. There was a Russian thinker, Peter

Kropotkin, who wrote *Mutual Aid*. His theory did not get accepted because it did not suit the capitalist system. The capitalist system wants you to believe in the competitive survival of the fittest: the strong will survive, the weak will disappear. Nature is red in tooth and claw so humans have to be the same. That kind of capitalist interpretation of nature is not correct. Soil supports the tree, the tree is transformed soil; sun and rain support the tree, the tree supports the soil by shedding its leaves. Earthworms support the soil, keep it fertile. Entire nature is co-operative. So, I think nature is benign, co-operative.

As I have already accepted, a certain amount of violence is there, but that is sacred because life gives life to maintain life. But within that life maintenance, life also supports life. Therefore, life gives life, takes life, supports life.

There are many new scientists who are saying that our old science is no longer viable. Ecological balance, sustainability, nature and human relationship have to be built on a completely new science. We have this new scientific interpretation of nature, but we teach old science in the universities in India. Whereas Western countries are now dropping the old science and getting into new science. Earth is a living organism, and there is a mutuality, reciprocity, which maintains nature. The new science is that of Gaia, Lovelock, Margolis, Capra...

I: Is India not in step with this movement? Gandhi advocated drawing upon the cultural traditions of the country. Today we have popular yogis and gurus like Baba Ramdev, Sri Sri Ravishankar and maybe Jaggi Vasudev who are selling some traditional products but they are more or less all into the same world of material prosperity of some kind ... whereas Gandhi was really talking about setting up a village-based civilisation.

Satish: I am not fully familiar with the work of Sri Sri Ravi Shankar. I have met him. And I'm not familiar with Ramdev. And did you mean Sadhguru Jagdish? I met him as well in London, we were staying with the same host. They are trying to bridge the material business world on the one hand with the spiritual world on the other. Because they see Unilever, Tatas and Ambanis, and such types of businesses as completely Westernised and deprived of spiritual content. They think in order to respond, they need to create something which can answer these corporations and yet has some cultural roots in India and Indian philosophy, Ayurveda, yoga and so on.

I will give them the benefit of the doubt, maybe they have good intention and motivation, and I would like to see them more small-scale, decentralised and not so money-oriented. But still, they are trying to bring something different. And in a way, I don't need to spend my time fighting somebody like Ramdev and Sri Sri Ravi Shankar. I will spend more time fighting the Tatas, Ambanis, Unilever ... not so much Unilever, but Tesco and BP and all those big multinational corporations. When you have a movement, you have to allow, I would like to allow and accept and respect, many different approaches within the movement. If you become too narrowly focused on only one way, then it becomes very sectarian.

For example, our alternative environmental Sarvodaya movement is quite disunited. People, even Vandana Shiva or Manish Jain or people like that, are working their own little fields and insist that theirs is the only way. I would like a little more unity and allowing of different expressions of the same vision and philosophy. I do not know enough about Ramdev and Sri Sri Ravi Shankar's work so I cannot 100% say whether they are good or not, but I would give them the benefit of the doubt, and I would say at least they are not exactly the same paradigm as the industrialised, centralised, mechanised, materialistic world view. They are doing something more healthy, more ecological, organic. Sri Sri Ravi Shankar sends his people here for learning the organic way of farming. The Dalai Lama sends Tibetans here to learn organic farming.

Even if they are going a little bit in the right direction, if Unilever is doing a little bit in the right direction, then it is better than completely 100% industrialised type of work. One Brazilian woman asked me today whether, if a big business needed to experiment with some new ideas but could not afford to stop its existing business, but gave us 10 million dollars for a new project which is more experimental, more organic, more ecological, more sustainable, would we accept it? If they do not control us and it is an experiment, research in action, I would say it is a good idea.

I will not say, no, you are a big business, I won't take your money. Gandhi didn't do that, he took money from Bajaj and the Birlas. I would not like to be too puritan and too exclusive. I want the movement to be a bit bigger, more inclusive, with a bigger front, and a with little bit of variety, difference, disagreement, it doesn't matter, we can live with it. Even in Vinoba's *Bhoodan** movement, there were many shades of opinion.

We need to have one big goal, of creating an ecological and social justice movement. And with that goal, if you agree, even if there is a little bit of difference it does not matter. We need to be generous of spirit. Gandhi was generous in spirit. I heard Abdul Gaffar Khan [1890-1988, also known as the Frontier Gandhi for his advocacy of non-violence] came to Sevagram, and Gandhi allowed him to eat meat.

I: That's right. He asked people to cook it for him.

Satish: Exactly. That was his generosity of spirit. Gandhi was a vegetarian, but he said Badshah Khan is not a vegetarian, let us allow him to eat meat. So that kind of generosity of spirit I would like to see in our movement. We should be more united and we should not be too judgemental within the movement, because we have a bigger calling and a bigger opponent, and that bigger opponent is the industrial, materialistic, consumerist society which is anthropocentric and does not care for nature and does not care for the poor. I want to stand against them and whoever is standing with us with even a few differences, I will accept him or her.

I: So, if Monsanto gives 10 million dollars do you think Vandana Shiva should take it? She will say – no way.

Satish: Vandana will say no, but I will say there are certain conditions. They must be sympathetic to your work. They may say we are doing this but, Vandana, your seed saving is a very good idea, it is an experiment. Whether you succeed or our seeds succeed we don't know. Let's try both. But we want to try your work. Genuine, sincere, authentic sympathy. I would say in that case Vandana should accept it.

I: But isn't there the danger that this kind of process has a way of taking you into the system, co-opting you? Even if you are credible, you may be lending legitimacy to something, some other actions that the funder does.

Satish: Not necessarily. I take money for *Resurgence* at Schumacher College from people who are millionaires or billionaires in Hong Kong or in London, to support our bursary programme. But there is no co-option. They believe in what we are doing. Like Bajaj and Birla believed in what Gandhi did, although Birla didn't change, he remained Birla and he remained a businessman. But he did not co-opt Gandhi.

Birla and Bajaj did not want to exploit Gandhi. Gandhi was supported by them, but Gandhi never supported them in their business. So Vandana will not support Monsanto ever, but Monsanto can support Vandana. That's how a new experiment can happen.

Buddha was given money by very wealthy people. There is the story of the merchant who wanted to buy a *jetavana*, a monastery, for Buddha, and he asked the king how much money he wanted. The king was very greedy and said, 'You pave the land with the gold, whatever amount of land you can pave with gold, you can have that land.' So he paved five or ten acres of land with gold, to create a *jetavana* for Buddha, and Buddha accepted it. But Buddha was not compromised. Buddha did not support the merchant, the merchant was supporting Buddha.

The Nobel Peace prize is given from money earned from dynamite, something unpeaceful. If Wangari Maathai or the Dalai Lama gets the Nobel Peace Prize, I would not oppose it. But if they give the peace prize to the wrong person, whether the money has come from a good source or a bad source, they are giving it to the wrong person. That is the kind of wisdom and judgement you need to make.

Chapter 12:

On Beauty, Speed and iPhones

Can we escape modernity? Is not an iPhone an object of beauty for a teenager, who can connect, call and open a whole new world of communications and content with it? Yes, says Satish Kumar, but durability is important. Make an iPhone and let it last and last, like his rice cooker which has been in use for the last 35 years and works fine even today.

I: How long have you been living in Devon?

Satish: I have been there for 35 years. I was in London before that – for five to six years. My wife June and her mother had a house in London, so we lived there, but we found London too much. June also wanted some land, and we got a couple of acres, and we now grow our food. There are 15 apple trees. We grow a lot of our vegetables and fruit. I come out of the house and the land and all these trees are like paradise. For me, living in a city is hell. But people think that living in Mumbai is better than living in Kachchh.

I: How have you managed your household, given your background as a monk, your ideas, thinking and approach to living?

Satish: I try to take a middle path. I am not an extreme Jain any more. I live in a kind of very austere way. I have managed to keep my life simple, and grow as many vegetables as I can in my two-acre garden, and I am very fortunate that for 45 years I have lived with June, my wife, and she is amazingly spiritual, has a Buddhist practice of meditation, and is a great gardener. So we have a good partnership. And we are very fortunate to have two very enlightened children. Or son Mukti and our daughter Maya are both very ecological, spiritual, frugal. They meditate, and both of them have been to Goenka's *Vipassana* [a type of Buddhist meditation] and they follow that path. My wife June goes to Plum Village in France. She has been going there for the last 15-20 years. And she also has a meditation practice. So, in our household, we are all following similar paths, although they are not the same. So be it *Vipassana,* be it inter-being, be it Jain or Gandhian, we are all ecological, spiritual, frugal, living a simple life. That is my household.

I: Do your children pursue what you do?

Satish: My son has a small organisation which promotes insulation of houses in order to reduce energy consumption and carbon emission. My daughter teaches dance, and she has a seven-year-old child. So June and I are grandparents. We have a very conducive family atmosphere. They are both very kind to us and we love them.

I: Where are you by Western standards, in terms of per capita income, or in terms of the kind of life that you are leading. Would you be called middle class, lower middle class … ?

Satish: This is again a label. It is very difficult to define what middle class, etc., is, because those distinctions are about 15 years out of date. I would say my income and expenditure would be closer to maybe lower middle class. I don't know, it is very difficult to define.

I: I am going back to this idea of voluntary poverty. From Jesus to Gandhi, they have argued for it.

Satish: I call it elegant simplicity. I don't use the term voluntary poverty for my own life. I say I practise elegant simplicity, by which I try to minimise waste, I try to have everything in the house beautiful, useful, durable and minimal, as far as possible. That is the ideal that I pursue and practise – elegant simplicity.

I: Does that cost? Does elegant simplicity cost you something?

Satish: No. It is a kind of taste, a sense, it is not material. And durability is very important. My son feels the same. If you are getting something, think how long it will last. If you have a choice between something that will last for five years and something that will last for 20 years, even if the thing that will last 20 years costs you a little more, my son and I and June will say that it is better to have that rather than having it reproduced again. I use a rice pot. I've been using that rice pot for the last 35 years, and that will last me my whole life and then it will be inherited by my children and grandchildren. It can last for generations, the same rice pot. I have a cooker. The last cooker I had lasted 70 years and then it broke. I phoned the company that made the cooker and they came and said it would not work anymore. So I had to get a new cooker. I decided to get a similar cooker so it would last another seventy, eighty, or 100 years, for generations. So that is the idea of elegant simplicity, where things should last.

Consider houses, we live in a house that is 400 years old and it will last another 400 or 500 years. It is beautiful to look at, it is a stone house and it will last for generations. For modern houses, they give a guarantee for 30 or 40 years, and they don't last longer. So, making something to last is part of elegant simplicity.

I: Yes, you have described that in your book. But what you see is beautiful from your perspective. A boy of eighteen or twenty sees an iPhone as beautiful, and what do you tell him?

Satish: I say make an iPhone and give a guarantee that it will last for ten years and I will be happy. Then work for 10 years to produce another iPhone that is so good it will last another 10-15 years, but don't just keep changing your phone every year or every other year.

I: But 2G goes to 3G to 4G to 5G and we and get faster transmission speeds.

Satish: But why do we have to go so fast? Where are we going with these speeds? You used to use an iPhone which would take maybe five minutes to get going, but now it will take three minutes or two minutes. But so what. People are building a railway from London to Birmingham, a whole new high-speed railway, and how much time will it save? Twenty minutes. And what are you going to do in those 20 minutes, are you going to take the name of God or write some beautiful poetry or read Shakespeare? No, you are going to do something as bad, as you do now.

So, without wisdom, if we progress in technology, it is not going to bring us any great satisfaction or contentment, or fulfilment or joy. But if you have wisdom together with technology, then technology does not become your master. Your wisdom is your master and you know how to use technology in a wise way, which is not wasteful, polluting and destructive. And so, the progress of wisdom and science and technology should go hand in hand.

For my life, I call it elegant simplicity. I am working on a new book, which will be titled *Elegant Simplicity,* or something like it.

I: It is said that we are now preparing for the next revolution, which consists of artificial intelligence, machine learning, 3D printing ... shop floors will have no people. And this is a reality that is coming. We already have robots, and jobs will disappear.

Satish: And then what? Why are we doing it? In the modern world, people know how to do things but they don't know why they do them. I teach them if possible, but mostly remind them, that yes, you know how to do things, how to make some amazing technology, amazing artificial intelligence, amazing robots, how to build them. But do you ask why you are doing all this? What is the purpose, and also what is the result of it and the consequences? How much resources will it take, what will be the effect on people? Just knowing that something can be done and therefore you do it, that is not enough. And this is why you need wisdom.

I: How would you take this to the next generation – your vision, your life experiences?

Satish: At Schumacher College, we bring young people together for ten days and explore ... You cannot guide them by holding their hand, you can just inspire them.

I: The problem in India is a little different, we have the problem of poverty, we have a GDP growth to attain, to meet the poverty.

Satish: Poverty and deprivation do not go away by economic growth, they go when you share. And there is no sharing in India. Businessmen and industrialists accumulate in the banks, in the stock market, they are investing all over the world, in China, in Germany, everywhere. India is not poor because we do not have economic growth but because we are mean, we don't share.

When we employ a coolie at a railway station and he asks for Rs 300 we want to give him Rs 200. The coolie is not going to make millions if we give him Rs 100 more and it is not going to break your pocket – why are you haggling with a coolie? You take a rickshaw and the man asks for Rs 50 and you say you will give him Rs 20. What is Rs 50 for you and me, but it is important for that poor man. We don't share, we always bargain for a few rupees. So, poverty will not go away ever, 500 years hence, 1,000 years hence, unless we are prepared to share.

America is not a happy society even though it is the number one economy. England is not a happy society although it is the number five economy, Germany is not a happy society. There is more happiness in Norway, Denmark, Sweden, because they are sharing more. They are socialist societies. They have high technology, they are very rich and they share. They have child benefit, old-age benefit, pension, unemployment benefit, housing benefit, free transport – everything is shared, so they are happy. You will not find so much poverty in Sweden. But in America, there is no lack of poverty. There are millions of people without food, without education, without medicine; health problems are acute.

So in India, [Prime Minister Narendra] Modi might be dreaming that we will get GDP growth of 10% or 15% more and the poverty will be gone. It will not go. Poverty will only go when you are prepared to share. Where there is a lot and it is not shared, there is poverty.

Entropy, the human predicament

Satish: The problem is entropy. When great idealists like Jesus Christ, Buddha, Mahatma Gandhi, start something, and then energy runs out (among the lot continuing their legacy) that is entropy. When energy runs out, idealism runs out, and the Christian Church becomes an establishment, as does the Buddhist temple. Gandhians, too, lose their idealism and become influenced by others who take over. That is a kind of human predicament. So, every time, in every age, you need refreshing and renewing of the spirit, which was like Jesus Christ or Buddha, Mahavir, Mahatma Gandhi, Martin Luther King, Nelson Mandela. What is happening in South Africa? Where is Nelson Mandela's spirit? Already, within 10 years, it is going. Obama coming to power, coming from the black community, where is Martin Luther King's vision? He (Obama) was very middle-of-the-way and mainstream.

So, entropy is to have that energy running out, idealism running out, and that is the human predicament. So, in every age, we need new impetus, new energy, new, refreshing ideals. That is why Vinoba came, J.P. Narayan [*1902-1979, Indian socialist leader noted for his call for a "total revolution" in the 1970s as he rallied forces against the policies of the then Indian Prime*

Minister, Indira Gandhi] came, now Vandana has come, in organic farming. So, always, you have to renew the spirit.

And you talk about science. The mainstream scientists have hijacked the original idea of science. Science meant simply knowledge. The original idea of science had nothing to do with empirical knowledge, measured knowledge or quantifiable knowledge. These are all added, as entropy, as a kind of deterioration set in, to exploit the word science. Science is simply knowledge and conscience. Conscience means knowing together. You and I share something and that becomes the conscience of a nation or the conscience of society. Language deteriorates, institutions deteriorate. This is nature, like a tree, which deteriorates in the winter and renews in spring. We have to always work on renewal. We have to accept the decay.

I: Is this predicament the destiny of the species?

Satish: Not destiny. It is the nature of our existence – birth, a bit of continuation, and then decay. The decay is part of nature, part of our universal design, if you want to call it that. Decay in the Gandhian movement, in the Buddhist movement, the Christian movement, in all the great movements ... decay happens, so the new generation has to renew them, revive them, regenerate them, and in that way refresh them. So this is our responsibility, to renew and refresh.

I: To come back to the mainstream and non-mainstream. You find yourself in the minority. It has been said of Francis Bacon that the empirical investigations of his new method were not only passionate, but often outright vicious. Nature was bound into service and made a slave, put in constraints. The aim of the scientist was to torture out nature's secrets.

Satish: Steal the secrets of nature, torture them – that's Francis Bacon. You have human slavery, you have imprisonment of humans; in the same way you have imprisonment of nature. These scientists are saying that they have to put nature and animals in factory farms. Six thousand cows in one farm, milked by robots; they never see the light of the day in their entire life. That is torturing animals so that humans can have milk, cheap and quick and easy. So you can say that is mainstream. It is nothing but deterioration of the ideal. We always need to be alert and awake and fight. So, we the minority will always remain the so-called minority, at the fringe.

I: This (the mainstream way of life) is also termed pragmatism, and Gandhi is supposed to be a pragmatic idealist. How do we explain that?

Satish: I am a pragmatist-idealist but I am more idealist than pragmatic. People tell me that Gandhi was not a realist so much as an idealist, although he himself said he was an idealist-realist and an idealist-pragmatist. People tell me that I am too idealistic, and it is not going to work in mainstream society. And I say, tell me what the realists have achieved. What have they got to show us? After 200 to 300 years of capitalism, industrialism and materialism, research and technology, and all the things we have created, the realists' systems have not been able to address any problem or deliver any lasting solution. Poverty has not gone, wars have not gone, conflicts have not gone, the Middle East is in turmoil, America is in poverty and disarray. What have the realists achieved? In spite of all the wealth and technology and science, we have not solved either human problems or the problems of our relationship with nature. Realists had enough chance and enough time to do something but they have not been able to succeed. Instead of success, they have given us more problems, bigger problems. There is more plastic in the oceans today than fish.

I: Why are they called realists?

Satish: So if you are a realist, you measure (what is 'real', what relates to things). Materialists and realists are of one type. Idealists are visionary. This table is real because it can be measured. You make a rule, and that is a measure. You come at 9 o'clock exactly. Drona [the programme manager at Dehradun] says this is a rule, sharp time, so he is a realist. But the idealist is flexible – it doesn't matter if you come five minutes early or five minutes late. Don't worry, be polite, be kind, be gentle, don't force things, don't impose things, be polite – use *Vinaya* [prudence]; that is more important than fixed timings and order. So, realists are more rule-bound and measured and exact, while the idealists are a little bit more flexible, improvising, imaginative and creative, and they can bend the rules – that is the difference.

I: But the pragmatists become domineering and dominant and they set the rules of the game by which society runs.

Satish: What realists do want is apparent, more immediate, you can see it, and therefore it is accessible. The idealist is still rather vague, and somewhere you grapple to understand what he says. You can never really understand the ideals of Gandhi, Buddha, Jesus, the great thinkers and musicians and poets, Rabindranath Tagore. Their ideals are such that you have to grapple with them, you have to be courageous to understand them and you will never fully understand them. But realists are exact. Exactly 9 o'clock. This table should be three feet long and two feet wide, exactly.

I: So this solves a lot of problems.

Satish: It appears that this is a better way, but it is without imagination. Imagination, spirituality, idealism ... they are abstract and implicit, hidden, so people are not able to grasp them. But that is precisely where we need to look and go and engage for a life well lived, and to learn and grow.

A Road Open to All

By Jagdish Rattanani

This book marks the beginning of a series of longform conversations with people who have questioned accepted narratives, worked with alternative frameworks and shown the pathway to better living and flourishing, in harmony with nature. These are some of our tallest leaders and quietest workers, and their messages are important if we are not to be lost in a world overwhelmed by the din of what passes as modern-day development. Satish Kumar's is one such voice.

What do his words add up to?

Satish's life can be seen in the context of Action Research, a range of approaches that enable subjective experience and objective observation to sit at the table of knowledge as equals, opening new paths to grow in ways not limited by mere cognitive capacities. Satish's journey has been marked by questions that are no different from the questions many action researchers would ask: How can we change the situation for the better? How can we do this in association with, and with the active participation of, those in the given situation? How can we inquire in a self-reflective way and/or with others to open new ways of knowing and doing?

Preparing to be a Jain monk in his early years, Satish Kumar could see the incongruities around him – for example, armed volunteers protecting monks who preached an extreme form of non-violence, or a sense of being controlled by a strict order that could not answer the questions bubbling up in his mind as a teenager. This disquiet was among the triggers that led him to leave the order in a dramatic escape that was planned and executed following conversations with two equally young monks. Embracing the Gandhian thinking that religion does not mean escapism, he now explored living in the everyday world, not separate from it, but still a seeker. On the

25th anniversary of the remarkable experiment that grew to become Schumacher College, the place where students grow and cook their food and learn from nature, Satish wrote: "I want Schumacher College students to go out into the world and work for something greater ... work with imagination, work in the service of the Earth, and work for the values and ideals they hold dear in their hearts." (Kumar, 2016)

The approach emphasises action. It also recognises the agency of every participant, celebrates diversity of thought and seeks to participate in the process of knowledge-creation so that it is no longer the privilege of hallowed portals of universities and their methods. Data is among the people and so is knowledge.

An illustration of what such epistemological diversity can achieve is cited by Hilary Bradbury:

> *In the 1970s, Donald Henderson led the WHO team that eradicated smallpox. The vaccine predated the eradication by over a century ... Henderson however brought skill with cultivating collaborative networks, and was able to accord local knowledge the same weight as the original scientific advances in immunology. Combining insight and artistry, leadership and participation, he thus led in realizing a cure the world over.*
>
> (Bradbury-Huang, 2015).

Reflecting on his work, Henderson wrote:

> *In the evolving new world of medicine, it seems to me that the assurance of a satisfactory patient-physician relationship is para-mount. Might relationship not be more productive if it incorporated stronger motivations for physicians to be more greatly concerned about continuity in the care and maintenance of health in their patients, about patient satisfaction and confidence in the physician, and about measurements and the assurance of quality? The first two of these concepts remind us of values embodied in the old family practitioner and the last echoes our belief in medicine being, at least in part, a science. A patient-physician relationship based on these premises ought to prove more rewarding than most such encounters today.*
>
> (Henderson, n.d.)

The vaccine was a breakthrough but no less a breakthrough was getting it to work in a world "under the most impossible of conditions" (University of Rochester, 2020).

In other words, the technology could not deliver fully till it was enmeshed with an understanding of, and an engagement with, people, cultures, policies, politics, economics and the complex interplay of these forces. By breaking the observer-observed boundaries, by listening to a wide range of voices, by learning from experience, it was possible to discover richer dimensions of knowledge and translate it into results that were remarkable.

In this approach, living bristles with opportunities to learn, grow and change the world in ways not possible when knowledge is the privilege of a closed-doors laboratory. We are all co-inquirers in the journey of life. We are encouraged to experiment, to ask, to explore and help create new awareness. We can learn to ask what William Torbert has called "good questions", which are "intrinsically valuable because they heighten our awareness, make us more alive and more related to the rest of our own lives and everything else" (Torbert, 1994). Allowing such questions to bubble up and reflecting on them forms what Action Researchers call the "inner arc of attention", aided by an "outer arc" that raises these questions with others and invites action in the world.

Discarding the comfort and security of money, Satish Kumar joined E. P. Menon on a global walk to meet world leaders and ask for nuclear disarmament. It was an impossible idea. But it worked. His journey was full of memorable stories and experiences that have helped define the change that he and E.P. Menon have led in their own ways. Satish Kumar acted.

Our questions and actions, small and big, can chart the road, build experiences and form the basis of work that helps us learn and grow in harmony with the human and more-than-human world of which we are a part. Knowledge becomes "a living, evolving process of coming to know rooted in everyday experience", of "transformation of our experience in conversation with the self and others", thus enabling "useful actions that leave us and our co-inquirers stronger" (Reason & Bradbury, 2008).

This also leads us to the understanding that the so-called experts may not know it all. We can challenge the academics, debate with the policy makers, revisit their theories, models and research to build new knowledge that is lived and felt. We can revel in an extended epistemology that recognises all forms of knowledge – propositional knowing, practical knowing, experiential knowing and presentational knowing. We can learn and know from theories, from doing, from experience and from art forms.

The extended epistemology of co-inquiry is the foundation for the belief that "good research is research conducted with people rather than on people" and that "ordinary people are quite capable of developing their own ideas and can work together in a cooperative-inquiry group to see if these ideas make sense of their world and work in practice" (Heron & Reason, 2014). It helps set the ground for inquiry that can challenge set thinking and learn from what we can together discover.

This is also a path to unleashing a new wave of creativity and innovation for a new way of living and working. A student of economics can ask if rising consumerism and GDP growth are meaningful measures of development, and if what is taught in theory ties up with lived experience, just as a business leader can begin to question practices that place a green label on products, services and processes that are anything but green.

As we look wider and enrol co-inquirers from all walks of life, we can open the path to giving voice and meaning to the everyday struggles of everyday people, to the anguish of those left out of the debate and help create a culture of inquiry of the kind Satish Kumar has conducted all his life. In doing this, we are in service to ourselves, our co-inquirers, and the universe of which we are a part. We can call this our abundant love.

References

Bradbury-Huang, H. (2015). 'Introduction: How to Situate and Define Action Research'. In H. Bradbury (Ed.), *The Sage Handbook of Action Research* (3rd ed., 2015, pp. 1-10) Sage Publications

Henderson, D. A. (n.d.). Donald A. Henderson, M.D. 'Class of '54 – Alumni Class Reflections', Univ. of Rochester Medical Center. https://bit.ly/Satish13

Heron, J. & Reason, P. (2015). 'Extending Epistemology within a Co-operative Inquiry'. In H. Bradbury (Ed.), *The Sage Handbook of Action Research* (3rd ed., 2015, pp. 366-380) Sage Publications

Kumar, S. (2016). 'Schumacher College at Twenty-Five'. *Resurgence and Ecologist Magazine*. Issue 298, Sep/Oct 2016

Reason, P. & Bradbury, H. (2008). 'Introduction'. In P. Reason & H. Bradbury (Eds.), *The Sage Handbook of Action Research – Participative Inquiry and Practice* (2nd ed., pp. 1-10). Sage Publications

Torbert, W. R. (1994). 'The Good Life: Good Money, Good Work, Good Friends, Good Questions', *Journal of Management Inquiry*, 3(1), 58-66

University of Rochester (2020). 'Eradicating smallpox: A Rochester-trained scientist led the way'. https://bit.ly/Satish14

GLOSSARY

This glossary is not to be taken as a full and formal reference for the entries listed here. It is meant to offer a brief overview of selected references to enable readers to place them in context.

Aiteraya Brahmana: One of the two Brahmanas of the Rig Veda, the earliest of the four Vedas, themselves the earliest known body of Indian scripture. Brahamanas may be considered as commentaries on the hymns contained in the Vedas.

Ambar charkha: A more efficient model of the hand-cranked wooden spinning wheel for making yarn from cotton. It was introduced by Gandhi in the mid-1900s with the help of some technologists. During the Independence movement, Gandhi encouraged Indians across India to make hand-spun yarn to reduce dependence on British mills. The charkha became a symbol of resistance to foreign rule.

Dr B.R. Ambedkar (1891-1956): An Indian leader from the oppressed Dalit communities, which were considered 'untouchable'. He studied in the USA, England and Germany with the help of a scholarship from the Maharaja of Baroda (today Vadodara in Gujarat). Upon his return, whatever he tried his hand at – consultancy, legal practice, teaching – he faced humiliating discrimination at the hands of the upper castes. He led several movements among his community – such as to secure entry into temples or to access wells for drinking water in the villages. In the end, he rejected Hinduism altogether and converted to Buddhism, taking along to the new faith a large chunk of his community in the state of Maharashtra, where he hailed from. He had a leading role in the drafting of India's Constitution.

Ananda Coomaraswami (1877-1947): A man of Sri Lankan and British parentage who was an art historian and among the earliest to interpret and analyse Indian and Sri Lankan art and culture in Western terms. He has written extensively on these subjects.

Anekanta: In Sanskrit, instability, uncertainty. In Jainism, a principle denoting the multiple and relativistic nature of reality.

Annapurna: Literally, 'full of food' in Sanskrit. Annapurna is also one of the names for Shiva's wife and is the goddess of plenty/harvests/food/the kitchen.

Aparigraha: One of the five yamas (guidelines for the conduct of one's life) in yoga, meaning not attached to possessions, not grasping, willing to let go. A concept in Jainism too.

Arambh: Start, beginning, inception.

Bhagavad Gita: Literally 'song of God'. Considered the most holy scripture of the Hindus. It is a dialogue between the warrior Arjuna and his charioteer Krishna, who is actually an avatar of the god Vishnu. Repulsed at the thought of fighting and killing, Arjuna throws down his arms just as the war of the Mahabharata, a fight between two sets of cousins, is about to start. In the dialogue that follows, Krishna tells Arjuna about what makes for right action and right understanding, the purpose of life and the nature of the divine, in the end convincing him that it is his sacred duty to fight a just battle.

Bhajans, kirtans: Both are devotional compositions in praise of a particular deity, set to music. Kirtans often involve the audience and are an 'exchange'. The main singer delivers a line, calling out to the audience to repeat it. There are slight regional differences in India in the use of these terms.

Bharatanatyam: An Indian classical dance form that evolved in the state of Tamil Nadu.

Bhoodan: Literally, 'donation of land'. In the *Bhoodan* Movement initiated by Vinoba Bhave, a disciple of Gandhi, wealthy landowners were persuaded to give up a portion of their land for the landless.

Bindi: A coloured dot worn in the middle of the forehead by Indian women, especially Hindus. It can be decorative or religious. Various meanings have been attributed to it, one being that it is worn on the site of the ajna chakra, positioned between the eyebrows, which represents the seat of wisdom.

Bodhgaya: A place in the state of Bihar in India and one of the most sacred pilgrimage centres of the Buddhists. This is where the Buddha is believed to have attained enlightenment, sitting under a bodhi (peepal, *Ficus religiosa*) tree. The chief site of worship here is the Mahabodhi temple complex.

Castes (Brahmins, Kshatriyas, Vaishyas, Sudras): Ancient Hindu society had four chief castes: *Brahmins,* who were priests and teachers; *Kshatriyas,* the warriors and rulers; *Vaishyas,* the merchant and trading classes; and *Sudras,* those who did manual labour. It is believed that at one time people could switch castes when their professions or vocations changed, but later the divisions became very rigid.

Chappals: The word for sandals in India, roughly resembling flip-flops in design.

Charaiveti charaiveti: Literally an exhortation meaning 'Keep walking, keep walking', it actually refers to the endless journey towards self-realisation, along which one never stops.

Charkha: A hand-cranked wooden spinning wheel used in India to spin cotton into yarn. It became a major symbol of defiance during the days of the Indian Independence movement, when Gandhi persuaded people to boycott foreign cloth.

Chaturmas: Literally, 'four months'. It refers to the monsoon period of four months, considered holy and suitable for retreat. Laypersons may perform various austerities, fast, or follow a vow for that period. For sanyasis (those who have given up mainstream life for spiritual pursuits and wander about the countryside) Chaturmas meant a 'monsoon retreat', when they stopped their wanderings and lived in one place, spending their time in prayer and meditation, and sometimes preaching among the people around.

Dalit: A term for a range of castes which were considered untouchable. The word was first used by the Maharashtrian reformer Jyotirao Phule in the 1930s. At the time, it was used as a Hindi/Marathi translation for 'depressed classes'. The word is also thought to have its roots in Hebrew, the language in which 'dal' means oppressed.

Derasar: The word for Jain temple in western India.

Deshatan: The touring of 'another country'; wandering through regions other than one's own.

Dharmashala: Rest-house for pilgrims. The name comes from Sanskrit and is a mix of dharma (virtue) and shala (house). The internationally known Dharamshala in the Northern Indian State of Himachal Pradesh, where the exiled Dalai Lama now lives, gets its name from here.

Gandhi-Nehru debate of 1945: On Oct. 5, 1945, Gandhi wrote to Jawaharlal Nehru, who later became India's first Prime Minister, to say: "I am convinced that if India is to attain true freedom and through India the world also, then sooner or later the fact must be recognised that people will have to live in villages, not in towns; in huts not in palaces. Crores (1 crore = 10 million) of people will never be able to live at peace with each other in towns and palaces. They will then have no recourse but to resort to both violence and untruth." Nehru replied: "A village, normally speaking, is backward intellectually and culturally and no progress can be made from a backward environment. Narrow-minded people are much more likely to be untruthful and violent."

Gram swarajya: Literally translates as 'village self-governance'. A term coined by Gandhi for his vision for India, of every village becoming a self-sustaining unit.

Gramdani: The relinquishing of privately owned land by villagers, or a group of villagers, in favour of communal ownership of the land. It was Vinoba Bhave, a disciple of Gandhi, who mooted the concept. Individual states have laws providing for formal establishment of 'Gramdan Villages'.

Grihastha ashram, vanaprastha ashram, sanyasa ashram, etc: The four stages of life prescribed in the ancient texts for an ideal Hindu man. Brahmachari-ashram sees him celibate and devoted to acquisition knowledge of the Vedas and other scriptures/skills associated with his caste; in Grihashta ashram, he is a worldly man, making a living, marrying and raising a family; in Vanaprashta ashram (literally meaning forest-dwelling stage), he retreats from active life, spending his time in prayer and pilgrimage; and in Sanyasa ashram, he leaves home, wife and family and goes away into the wilderness, to spend the rest of his life seeking self-realisation.

Gurukul: 'Home of the guru' – an institution where students live close to, and often in the home of, their guru, somewhat like a boarding school, for years together, till they are proficient in the scriptures/art/craft/profession they have come to learn.

Harijan: Of unsure provenance, meaning 'children of God', it was a controversial term used by Gandhi for the 'untouchable' castes. He ran a publication by the name of *Harijan* too. Dalit groups, as well as Ambedkar himself, objected to the use of the word. They found it condescending and offensive that instead of changing upper-class attitudes, their identity was being tinkered with instead. The Supreme Court of India, hearing a case in 2017, remarked that *Harijan* was a word of insult, and it is no longer used in official communication.

Hind Swaraj: Meaning 'Indian Home-Rule', this is a book written by Mahatma Gandhi in the form of a fictional dialogue between a reader and an editor of a journal. The book contains Gandhi's ideas on a range of topics – nationhood, development, modernity, society, religion, education etc.

Jain: Adherent of Jainism, a religion founded in India by Mahavira in the fifth or sixth century BCE. Jains believe in the attainment of self-realisation or enlightenment through a path of strict non-violence.

Karma yoga: One of the three paths to self-realisation in Hinduism, through selfless action or work, without concern for the results or fruits of action. The other two paths are Bhakti yoga, where man attains salvation through devotion and surrender, and Jnana yoga, where man arrives at self-realisation through knowledge and honest intellectual rumination.

Karnatic/Carnatic music: The classical music form of south India. The classical music of north India is referred to as Hindustani music. Both are based on ragas.

Karuna: Mercy, compassion.

Kathakali: An Indian classical dance form – or rather dance-drama form, involving music, dance, mask, pantomime and a trace of the martial arts – from the south-western state of Kerala.

Katla: Killing, decapitation.

Khuda: God. Originally a Persian word, but used by people in the Muslim belt from Turkey to India.

Kothewali: A prostitute in a brothel.

Mahabharata: An Indian epic dating back to the 4th century BCE and even earlier by some accounts; the longest work of literature in the world. The poetic composition tells the story of cousins at war and opens up many inquiries into what constitutes right action. The deep messages of the epic are presented at the climax in a conversation known as the Bhagavad Gita, the 'song of God'.

Moksha: (in religion) Release from the cycle of birth, death and rebirth occasioned by karma; (in general) liberation.

Mukta: Freed, liberated

Nai Talim/Bunyadi Talim: A system of 'basic education' conceived by Gandhi, where students would be taught in their mother tongue and would learn life skills and socially productive activities, apart from the standard subjects taught in regular schools.

Naxalite: Member of any of the armed revolutionary separatist groups in India with allegiance to Maoist communism. The term comes from Naxalbari, a village in West Bengal where there was a peasant uprising against landlords in the late 1960s, after which a number of militant communist groups sprang up in the area.

Nehru-Gandhi debate of 1945: See Gandhi-Nehru debate of 1945

Nirvana: The state of freedom from all suffering, the ultimate goal of Buddhism.

Padayatra: Journey by foot, usually undertaken in pilgrimage. In modern India, it has come to mean a symbolic march by a person or group for a cause, political or social.

Parmatman: In Indian spirituality, the eternal or supreme or universal soul/spirit, as opposed to the **atman,** the individual soul/consciousness, which merges into the **Parmatman** upon liberation.

Purna: Complete, whole, fullness.

Purushartha: Object or purpose of human pursuit. In Hinduism, there are four purusharthas – Artha (economic good), Kama (pleasure), Dharma (righteousness) and Moksha (liberation).

Sadhaak: Practitioner. Some who follows a spiritual practice or way of life, or even the practice of an art.

Samarambh: Readiness to do something, preparation for an activity (usually auspicious or important).

Samashti: The state of being whole, complete; the collective whole, of which the aggregate parts are not different from the whole; universality.

Samsara: World; the cycle of birth, living, suffering, dying and rebirth.

Sarvodaya: Uplift of all; social and economic development of society as a whole, as conceptualised by Gandhi.

Sat-chit-ananda: The state of 'being', consciousness and bliss, or existence-awareness-bliss, as a description or nature of the sole ultimate reality offered in the Upanishads. It is the subjective experience of the ultimate. Several meanings have been ascribed to this term.

Scheduled caste: The official term in India for several castes that have been historically discriminated against and are now protected by the Indian government and given special rights and concessions.

Shanti Niketan: A university-town in West Bengal, founded by Debendranath Tagore, father of the Bengali poet and Nobel Prize winner Rabindranath Tagore as an ashram initially. Rabindranath established the Visva Bharati university here, which is known for its emphasis on the arts, humanities, culture, language and music. Shanti Niketan is also a popular spot, with its many art centres, museums, festivals and other cultural attractions.

Shloka: Verse, hymn or poem set to a meter.

Mrs Slade/Mirabehn/Meera Ben (1892-1982): Born Madeleine Slade, she was the daughter of a British rear-admiral. She left everything in England to become a disciple of Gandhi and join his Sabarmati Ashram, and towards his last years was one of his principal caretakers, very often travelling with him. She came to be known as Mira Ben, after the sixteenth-century Indian mystic poet and devotee of the god Krishna.

Srishti: Sanskrit word for creation. In religion it could mean universe, nature, the world.

Sutras:

Dashwaikalik Sutra: A short yet profound teaching, which explains simply and clearly that the highest practice for a Jain monk is to be the embodiment of non-violence, restraint and penance.

Uttaradhyen Sutra: An important Jain scripture containing instructions on religious principles and practices, chiefly meant for a young monk.

Acharang Sutra: An agama or canonical text in Jainism prescribing codes of conduct for a whole range of activities – from how a monk may ask for food, what kind of food he may eat, eating etiquette, specifications for the bowl he uses, his couch and his clothes, to the study of the scriptures and spiritual practices.

Swaraj: Literally, 'self-rule' in Sanskrit. It is said to have been used by the Hindu reformer Dayanand Saraswati first, but the term is best known for its use by Mahatma Gandhi as a slogan for 'home rule', or independence from foreign (British) domination.

Tantra: A general term for various practices in Hinduism and Buddhism that may be called esoteric, occult, magical or secret, involving mantra (chants), mandalas (sacred symbols) and even rituals involving sex. Scholars on the subject would disagree; they hold that this is a superficial Western understanding of Tantra, which actually encompasses a vast range of practices aimed at spiritual salvation.

Tapas: Practice of some kind of asceticism or discipline—such as fasting, breath control, living in seclusion, meditation—to purify oneself.

Tapasya: Practice of some kind of austerity, such fasting, meditation, silence.

Untouchables: Those belonging to the lowest castes in Indian society, whose very touch was believed to pollute others, who would then need to do ritualistic purification. Untouchables were not allowed to draw water from the same wells as the rest of society, not allowed to eat with them or mingle with them socially in any way, and in some regions they were not to be seen even crossing the paths of people from the higher castes.

Vaishnava: Member of a sect of Hindus that worships the god Vishnu – and his avatars, like Rama and Krishna – as the supreme being. (A Shaivite worships Shiva as the Supreme Being, while a Smarta is non-sectarian and worships all Hindu gods).

Vyakti: Person, individual.

Yagna: Worship, sacrifice, offering; a Hindu ritual still practised, involving the lighting of a fire and the chanting of sacred verses. The fire god, Agni, is considered the bridge between man and the gods being worshipped.

Yuga (Satya yuga, Treta yuga, Dvapara yuga, Kali yuga): One of the four epochs or ages of mankind in Hindu cosmology. In Satya yuga, mankind is innocent and full of virtue. But mankind loses its goodness, in each yuga becoming progressively more degraded until, in Kali yuga, the world becomes very bad and is destroyed. The entire cycle of yugas then starts again, from Satya yuga. It is believed that mankind is at present in Kali yuga.

ACKNOWLEDGEMENTS

A book is like a longish journey, made all the more enjoyable because of co-travellers – friends and those who become friends along the way. To those who worked on the book, to those who later read, re-read and helped edit it and to my countless teachers and guides who over the years shaped and moulded the thinking that led to the book, I owe a deep debt of gratitude. This is a long list of people to thank.

I begin with my wife Lekha Rattanani, my companion, fellow journalist and co-founder of the Foundation of The Billion Press. Lekha has been a tireless editor and is a strong supporter of the idea of longform conversations. She read the manuscript multiple times, offered endless edits and has been the force in the background that made this book happen.

My friends Sudarshan Iyengar and Lisa Pearson brought their passion and commitment to the book project. This meant that the interviews were arranged and executed seamlessly, the research went on alongside and, without any fuss, a manuscript came to be. It is a blessing to have had the opportunity to launch this book series with friends like Sudarshan and Lisa.

The interviews themselves were made possible because of the generous spirit of Navdanya and its renowned founder, Vandana Shiva. Situated in Dehradun, the idyllic setting in the Doon Valley in the foothills of the Himalayas, this was the place we stayed and conducted the interviews with Satish Kumar.

I am indebted to two very special teachers – Charles Eisenstein and Arun Maira. Both took time from their busy schedules, readily agreed and promptly delivered two gems that sit as forewords to the book. These two opening pieces lend special meaning to the conversations and set the tone for the book.

The cover design is the original work of Jyoti Sahi, a painter and writer in Bengaluru who very generously agreed to give his art for the book. The seed as the source of life depicted in the artwork offers a rather exciting cover for a book that celebrates the soil as the springboard of new life. Sahi runs an art ashram in Bengaluru that explores the relation of art to spirituality and is also home to an experimental primary and secondary school for village children called the Sita School.

I am grateful to several senior leaders, academics, activists and writers who read the manuscript and/or offered comments. Among them, I must specifically thank László Zsolnai, Director of the Business Ethics Center at the Corvinus University of Budapest and President of the European SPES Institute; Helena Kettleborough, Director at the Association of Sustainability Practitioners, UK (ASP, UK) and Lecturer in Sustainability at the Manchester Metropolitan University Business School, UK; Emily Ryan, alumnus of Schumacher College and ecological educator who works with The Land Institute, Universidad de la Tierra, the Global Diversity Foundation, Bioneers, and the Women's Earth Alliance; Gwyn Jones, Director and Wisdom Council member at the ASP, UK and guest lecturer at several UK universities and business schools in Global Sustainability and Social Enterprise. This book has taken some four years to publish. In that time, I have spoken to countless others on the project and some have offered their thoughts and feedback. I'm grateful to all of them.

Many rounds of edits and a host of other inputs that helped shape and refine the manuscript before and after it was sent to the publishers came from my friend and fellow journalist Kripa Raman. Kripa is meticulous, supportive of the idea of longform conversations and an activist who has worked quietly to support ideas of sustainable living.

This book would not have been possible without the generosity of Andrew Carey, an editor who supported the venture right from the beginning and has put in long hours advising, editing and getting the book out. My deepest thanks to Andrew and the publishing house of Triarchy Press. I hope the meaningful work in the area of Systems Thinking led by Triarchy Press will continue to serve us all at this critical time.

Jagdish Rattanani
October 2022

INDEX

ABOUT THE AUTHORS

Sudarshan Iyengar

Dr Sudarshan Iyengar is a Gandhian economist and a former Vice Chancellor (from 2005-2014) of Gujarat Vidyapith, in Ahmedabad, India, the university founded by Mahatma Gandhi in 1920. Sudarshan calls himself a social volunteer by disposition.

Sudarshan has also headed the Gujarat Institute of Development Research, Ahmedabad (1999-2004), the Centre for Social Studies, Surat (2004-05), and served as a Distinguished Chair Professor of Gandhian Philosophy (2016-2018) at the Indian Institute of Technology, Mumbai. He is a Director of the Gandhi Research Foundation Jalgaon, and a trustee at the Sabarmati Gandhi Ashram.

Sudarshan researches in the areas of the commons and natural resource development and management, non-government institutions and Gandhian thought and practice. He has published around 70 papers and articles and eight books. His 2016 book *In the Footsteps of Mahatma: Gandhi and Sanitation* by the Publication Division, Government of India, has been translated into Gujarati and Tamil. Sudarshan now works with Action Research in Community Health and Development (ARCH) in Western India.

Lisa Pearson

Lisa Pearson first met Satish Kumar whilst a sustainable horticulture apprentice at Schumacher College and participated in the Resurgence 50 pilgrimage in 2016. Lisa is a Social and Therapeutic Horticultural Practitioner, working for a charity in the UK for people's health and wellbeing.

Lisa has facilitated workshops with a creative arts-in-prisons project and voluntarily mentored young people in custody. The completion of the MSc (Sustainable Food and Natural Resources) continued Lisa's research interest in agroecology, the bond to nature and wellbeing.

Jagdish Rattanani

Jagdish Rattanani is a journalist, a faculty member at a leading Indian B-School (SP Jain Institute of Management & Research, SPJIMR) and a director of an Indian non-profit news company (Foundation of The Billion Press) that works with the mission of bringing to focus people less seen, voices less heard and perspectives less argued. Jagdish also sits on the board and the wisdom council of the Association of Sustainability Practitioners, UK.

After leading newsrooms for over two decades, Jagdish writes syndicated editorial columns for the Indian press and engages with MBA participants at SPJIMR, teaching and learning in areas like Ethics, Business & Society, Responsible Leadership and Communications. Jagdish calls himself a seeker and an explorer of the idea of good living with 3Cs: contribution, connectedness and compassion.

About the Publisher

Triarchy Press is an independent publisher of books that take a systems thinking approach to some of the most important issues of our time, including:

- Improving the way that we run certain kinds of organisations (schools, local government and public services – including police and health services)

- Improving the way that leadership, innovation and teamwork happen in all organisations

- Improving the way that we think about the future (whether it's scenario planning in a company, saving the planet from genocide, ecological disaster or societal collapse, or preparing for crisis)

- Improving the way that we structure economies, banking and financial systems.

This is the first in a series of Longform Conversations with some of the thought leaders of our time. The series is edited by Jagdish Rattanani and published by Triarchy Press.

www.triarchypress.net

Longform Conversations

Longform Conversations of the kind presented in this book were conceived by journalists Lekha Rattanani and Jagdish Rattanani first as an antidote to 'soundbite journalism', the trend towards news that is shortened and slickly packaged to offer an oversimplified summary of events.

The quick-fix story may have some merits in a busy world full of fleeting images but it does a disservice to the idea of unpacking complex socio-politico-economic issues. It can reduce the standard of the debate, keep audiences less informed and less equipped to take a stand.

Longform Conversations seek to celebrate a 30-hour (or even longer) conversation, not a 30-second soundbite. Here, we want to take time and space to listen to people to help draw out experiences, reflections and insights. We can raise doubts, revisit positions and understand multiple perspectives.

This book is the first in a series that will play with some of these ideas. Longform Conversations are presented in a Q&A format to enable a range of readers, including young audiences and students, go as deep they might wish into a subject or a nuanced position. As well as following the conversation from the start, readers have the opportunity to begin on almost any page, to pick up nuggets of the conversation, drop off and return when and where they may like.

www.triarchypress.net/conversations